# 10 *easy* stitches

---

## Embroider 30+ Unexpected Projects

### Alicia Burstein

---

**stash**BOOKS®

*an imprint of C&T Publishing*

Publisher: Amy Marson

Creative Director: Gailen Runge

Acquisitions Editor: Roxane Cerda

Managing Editor: Liz Aneloski

Editor: Kathryn Patterson

Technical Editor: Debbie Rodgers

Cover/Book Designer: April Mostek

Production Coordinator: Tim Manibusan

Production Editor: Jennifer Warren

Illustrator: Linda Johnson

Photo Assistants: Mai Yong Vang and Rachel Holmes

Style photography by Kelly Burgoyne, subject photography by Mai Yong Vang, and
how-to photography by Rachel Holmes of C&T Publishing, Inc., unless otherwise noted

Published by Stash Books, an imprint of C&T Publishing, Inc., P.O. Box 1456, Lafayette, CA 94549

Library of Congress Cataloging-in-Publication Data

Names: Burstein, Alicia, 1981- author.

Title: 10 easy stitches : embroider 30+ unexpected projects / Alicia Burstein.

Other titles: Ten easy stitches

Description: Lafayette, CA : C&T Publishing, [2019] | Includes bibliographical references.

Identifiers: LCCN 2018035514 | ISBN 9781617457555 (softcover : alk. paper)

Subjects: LCSH: Embroidery--Patterns.

Classification: LCC TT770 .B946 2019 | DDC 746.44041--dc23

LC record available at https://lccn.loc.gov/2018035514

Printed in the USA

10 9 8 7 6 5 4 3 2 1

## dedication

To Daniel, my other half. You keep me stable, inspired, and honest, and you make sure the doors are locked every night. I love you.

To my beautiful, funny, loving, challenging, goofy, intelligent children. You amaze me every day and give life purpose.

## Acknowledgments

There are so many people I want to give a thank-you, a virtual high five, and a shout-out to! In no particular order, here they are:

Everyone at C&T Publishing. I couldn't have written this book without that lovely group of people taking a chance on a new author with a simple idea. I can't wait to do it again!

I want to thank my artists who supplied their art to be used as patterns:

Daniel Presedo, my dear artist husband, who draws the most amazing trees.

Gabrielle Price, a fourteen-year-old artist, who drew the beautiful ladies in the Pretty Girl Handkerchiefs.

Angele Carter, owner of the FabricAndInk shop, who created the Emperor Penguin Pincushion pattern just for this book! Head to her Etsy store (fabricandink.etsy.com) and drool over her beautiful felt and stitch work.

To the companies that supplied me with some of the most amazing materials and tools I could have asked for, I thank you! Your generosity is greatly appreciated. Thank you, Andover Fabrics, Inc.; Aurifil; Cloud9 Fabrics; Colonial Needle Company; Dear Stella; Kreinik Mfg. Co., Inc.; Riley Blake Designs; and The ThreadGatherer.

The most inspirational person in my crafty career is, as it is for many, my mother. As a rowdy little girl with Betty Boop curls, I was five years old when my mom turned to teaching me cross-stitch. I started with the little kits that included the metallic frame/hoops, moved onto reading patterns, and eventually made my own designs. Without her patience in teaching me the joy of making something with needle and thread, this book may have never existed. Thanks, Mom!

# Contents

# The Fun Part—The Projects!  40

**WEAR IT**
**42**

43

**Feathered Jean Skirt**
*A simple jean skirt elevated by a gorgeous peacock feather*

46

**Winged Shoes**
*Small wing designs stitched on mommy-and-me shoes*

48

**Collar and Cuffs**
*A simple button-down dressed up with delicate flowers*

51

**Sweater Elbow Patches**
*Pretty mushroom and flower patterns on vegan leather*

54

**Stacking Bracelets**
*Easy, wearable leather-look bracelets*

57

**Heart Rhythm Workout Tank**
*A workout tank accented with a sinus heart rhythm*

59

**Constellation Mini Hoop Necklace**
*Tiny glowing constellations for necklace hoops*

61

**Trim a Men's Classic Shirt**
*Free-form trimming for men's button-downs*

63

**Under the Sea Baby Clothes**
*Baby items adorned with hand-stitched jellyfish and a little mer-bun*

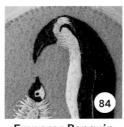

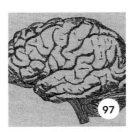
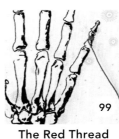

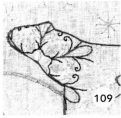

# Introduction

Welcome! I am so excited to share a long-term passion of mine and can't wait to see and get inspired by how other makers use this book.

I created this book to fill a void I found when looking for my own embroidery projects—the intermediate, quick-ish modern project that is just fun to do. When I would search for projects, they were either too complicated (I have an attention span issue), too kiddie, not complicated enough for my level, or not stylistically fun and interesting. So I set out envisioning projects that I got excited to make and that wouldn't take a month to finish.

## My Stitching Motto: "Be Free!"

My motto in art is "Be free!" When using this book, I encourage you to allow your creativity to be free and to release the control that can be ingrained in hand sewists. Each project has directions, but think of them as "guided suggestions." In fact, I purposely did not list which stitches and colors to use; it was *not* an oversight!

I want you to use your own ideas for stitches, your own color palettes, and your own creativity and style when doing these projects—or any project, for that matter. If you don't like the stitch used in the sample, then replace it with something you prefer. Use your favorites, learn something new, or experiment with different threads and weights. Go further and add beads to projects that don't call for them, try a color theme that you wouldn't normally choose, or try doing everything in inverse … you never know what will be amazing and inspire you.

## Interchangeable Patterns

I have always loved *sets* of things. You know, like my favorite teacup collection—I can't have just one, so I have to get *all* of them. You will find that some of the projects have multiple patterns that go together. These are provided for you to completely make a collection yours. Pick your favorite, or make all of them to give as a completed set.

I have also used basic, easy patterns so that many of them can be exchanged from one project to another and sized up or down and still make great projects. The Pretty Girl Handkerchiefs can be made into gorgeous hoops ready to hang, and why not make the appliqué nursery animals into quilt squares and make a matching blanket?

## The Advanced Beginner Assumptions

This book is not intended to teach basic fundamentals. The following are some assumptions I made when creating these projects:

1. You have sewn something before. Perhaps nothing extravagant or museum ready, but you know how to thread a needle, use an embroidery hoop, and understand the general basics of hand sewing.

2. You are familiar with basic sewing terms and phrases such as *right sides together* and *appliqué*.

3. You want to expand your current skills and aren't afraid of patterns that don't give explicit direction.

4. You have access to a computer and printer. (This is not required but will make projects much easier.)

5. You have used or are excited to use different materials and interfacings. Time to use up your stash!

# Learn It

*What we learn with pleasure we never forget.*
—Alfred Mercier

## Needles and Fabric and Thread, Oh My!

For this embroidery book, there are supplies you will need to have and then optional materials that are really nice to have. As many of you aren't true beginners, you may have at least a few of these lying around in your stash. If not? Well, I never pass up an excuse to go to the craft store!

### NEEDLES

Your needle is a staple in all types of hand sewing. I have so many but only use about one to two in each project (except for specialty stitches). Needles are easy to find and usually cheap. In fact, some of my favorites are the needles that come in hotel mending kits: They are average in size and length, sharp, and free.

Needles come in different lengths and thicknesses; the rule of thumb is the bigger the number, the thinner the needle. The thickness of a needle is important because it is what makes the hole in your material. For woven fabrics, this doesn't mean much, but if you are stitching on leather or plastic, you want to walk the fine balance of keeping the hole small and not hurting your thread. This isn't hard—it just takes a bit of practice.

Needles will be either sharp or blunt. For embroidery, you will almost always want a sharp needle because you need it to poke through the fabric. Blunt needles are used in cross-stitch on Aida cloth or while weaving so you don't pierce your threads, just wrap.

There are many types of needles, and each has some unique properties. Here are the top five that I use in most projects.

1. **Embroidery or crewel:** Sharp with a medium eye. This is the essential embroidery needle, and if you have to pick just one type, this is it.

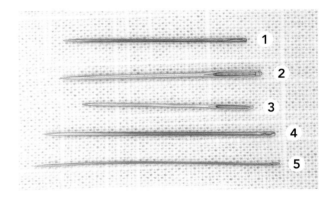

2. **Chenille:** Large and sharp with a long eye. These needles are great for larger threads and for threads that fray or are, in general, plain unruly (like metallic thread).

3. **Tapestry:** Blunt with a long eye. These are used for cross-stitch, needlepoint, and weaving when you don't want the needle to catch on the working thread or the fabric.

4. **Milliners or straw:** Long and sharp with a short eye. These needles are longer and have an eye that is the same thickness as the shaft, which is perfect for bullion knots and French knots.

5. **Beading:** Sharp with a short eye but *very* thin and long. These are a must for beadwork. Their size allows you to go through a bead with thread more than once. These will get some nice bends in them—that makes them even better.

### Four Ways to Thread Your Needle

This may seem self-explanatory, but there are a couple different ways to thread a needle.

**Method 1:** Put the ends of the thread through the eye of the needle. On the other end, either tie a knot or leave it free. Sew over it with the first few stitches.

**Method 2:** When using 2 strands of floss (or any even number), you can fold the strand(s) in half, put the free ends through the needle, and then use the loop to make a slipknot to start your stitching. This is my favorite!

**Method 3:** Same as above: Start with a single strand folded in half, but instead of putting both threads in the eye, only put one end through and run your needle to the middle of the thread. This will leave your needle on the thread without a dangly tail. This is great for metallic or satin thread because you don't have to worry about your needle falling off, and it seems to keep the strands more orderly.

**Method 4:** If you are working with a single strand, thread the needle only about one to two inches. Then poke the needle through the thread and tighten gently. This locks the single strand to the needle.

I rarely use method 3 or 4 because if I mess up I like to take my needle off the thread to pick out stitches. If the needle is attached to the thread, I have to cut it off, which annoys me. I will, however, always use method 3 for metallic thread because it is the easiest way to tackle the inherent unruliness.

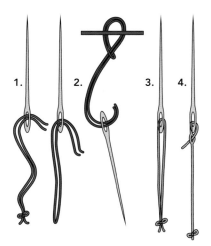

---

## Tips and Tricks for Needles

- You don't need a giant variety. I mainly use a long average-size embroidery needle, a very thin embroidery needle, and a beading needle for special projects.

- You will find a favorite needle. My very thin and sharp embroidery needle is now bent for my fingers from use over many hours. Don't be alarmed if you get a bend, as this makes them even better.

- You can use the little strawberry that is attached to the classic tomato pincushion to sharpen your needles. Yes—that really *is* what it's for!

- They have gold- and platinum-coated needles. I found there is a pretty negligible difference between these and my plain needles. For almost two to three times the cost, I personally don't find them worth it, but some stitchers really love them.

- If you need to do a weaving stitch like a whipped backstitch or a woven wheel, flip your sharp needle over and use the eye end to weave instead of getting a completely different needle! It works the same as a blunt tapestry needle and saves you from having to switch needles.

- Needles are magnetic, so keep a fridge magnet in your sewing box to keep pesky runaway needles contained.

## FABRIC

I am a fabric hoarder. I love, love, *love* all types of fabric and even keep old clothes if I think I can reuse some beautiful textile from them. Linen, quilt-quality cotton, denim, cotton knit, and felt are all great options, but don't stop there! Velvet, corduroy, silk, burlap, tulle, leather, vegan leather … the options are only limited by whether you can get a needle through it.

With embroidery, you can use almost anything as a base fabric. When displaying a project in a hoop, you have more flexibility because the fabric can be pulled taught and glued down. If you plan on making something loose like a pillow, a wallhanging, or clothing, there are some questions to ask before choosing the fabric.

1. **Will the fabric support the stitching?** You need to consider the heaviness of the stitching versus the weight of the fabric. You don't want to stitch a large solid pattern onto a thin fine-woven sweater. The fabric will pucker and stretch and sag, which is not the look we want. Heavy solid patterns need a sturdy background, such as linen, felt, high-quality quilting cotton, or interfacing.

2. **Will the thread show through your fabric?** If you are doing blackwork, it is shown off so well against a clean white or cream background. However, black thread can show through thin white fabric. Address this by finding a thicker white fabric or being careful about keeping your stitching super clean on the back. This means not trailing the thread across white space but instead tying off the thread and starting again. You can also lace your thread through stitches already placed to get your working thread to the place you need it to be. This also applies when stitching on tulle or lace.

3. **Do you need interfacing?** If you are sewing on clothes or stretchy material like cotton knits, you will need to use interfacing. Interfacing is a nonwoven, non-stretchy thin material that goes on the back of your fabric. It keeps knits from stretching and supports the stitches. Interfacing comes in many forms and thicknesses. If you are going to print your patterns onto wash-away pattern paper, this will work for interfacing *while* you are stitching, but if you need support after the project is finished, you will need a permanent option. I always use an iron-on or fusible interfacing; they are quick and easy to apply, and they don't need to be basted into place prior to starting.

The only problem I have run into with fusible interfacing was that I did not make sure the interfacing was *sew-through*, meaning that the glue was not too heavy to embroider through or too much trouble to sew through with my sewing machine. If you make the mistake of not getting sew-through interfacing and you have extra fabric, my suggestion (unfortunately) is to start again. If you can't start again, use silicone needle pullers and try different-size needles to see what works the best. Sometimes a finer needle will slip through it easier than a thick one. The glue can also stick to your needle and gum it up. Use the little strawberry attached to a classic tomato pincushion to clean and keep the needles sharp. If your needle feels too sticky, you can clean it with an alcohol wipe.

Fusible interfacing also comes double-sided. This is really great for firmly connecting two pieces of fabric together that you want to have extra support. Also be sure that this is sew-through!

*Quick tip:* Fusible *interfacing* is different than fusible *webbing*. Fusible interfacing is a fabric with glue on one or both sides. Fusible webbing is a thin, fine web of hot glue. Both are great at connecting two pieces of fabric, but the former adds support (excellent for knits!) and the latter simply combines fabrics (perfect for appliqué!). I have had some issues with fusible webbing coming apart after getting soaked or getting too hot, dissolving into the fabric, and not sticking. Just use some experimenting to get the heat right.

### Quilt-Quality Cotton

Go to any fabric store, and you will see bolt after bolt of stunning colors, patterns, and prints of cotton fabric. Some brands make nicer-quality fabric than others, but in general, 100% cotton fabric sews up well, holds creases, is colorfast, and comes in so many colors and prints that you can find fabric for anything. Because quilt cotton is a woven fabric, it will fray when cut unless backed with fusible interfacing or webbing. Cotton is also the best for iron-on appliqué due to its thin weight and tolerance of a nice hot iron. Some of my favorite brands of fabric are Cloud9 Fabrics, Dear Stella, Riley Blake Designs, and Andover Fabrics, Inc. They all have a gorgeous variety of patterns, and the fabric is great quality. What are your favorites?

### Felt

My favorite fabric hands down is wool-blend felt. I am not talking about the acrylic felt found at the craft store—I mean wool blended with rayon felt. It has a soft hand, doesn't fray, comes in *so* many colors, has gorgeous texture, holds embroidery stitches perfectly, and can be made into everything from toys to accessories to stunning lifelike flowers. Unfortunately, felt does have its limits: It is thick and bulky and so is not good for small necklaces and projects where the base has to be fine and flexible (use linen or cotton for that). I buy all my felt from Benzie Design (benziedesign.com), but there are many lovely felt makers to choose from.

## Linen

Linen is a lovely material to work with for hooped projects, as it has a luxurious finish and thickness. It is made up of a loose weave of flax strands, which create tiny holes in between. In addition to its pretty finish, it is perfect for making grid patterns, even lines, and satin stitches because you can keep the stitches lined up using these holes. I have heard from some that they don't like the nubby finish, so that is a personal taste. You can decide.

Due to its looser weave, linen also likes to shift and pull. In addition, its texture doesn't always allow the wash-away pattern stabilizer to stick to it as well as some other materials. Because of this, if I will have to move my hoop around even twice, I loosely run a basting stitch around my pattern before starting to make sure the pattern doesn't shift when moving a hoop or retightening the fabric. After you're done with the project, simply remove the basting stitch and wash away the pattern. I learned the hard way once: When halfway through a large project, I realized that one side of my stitching was 2″ from where it was supposed to meet the other side!

## Leather Look-Alikes

I love the look of real leather but not the price. Leather is also so thick that stitching more than a few straight stitches just isn't realistic. Lucky for me (and you!) there are so many other options available that imitate the look and feel of leather. Synthetic leather (also known as *vegan leather*) is a wonderful material to embroider on and use as a full base material or as accents. Needles go through most vegan leather with ease. It comes in some really gorgeous finishes, and it adds a feel of luxury to your finished projects.

Another option is kraft-tex (by C&T Publishing). This wonderfully thin and rugged kraft paper fabric looks, feels, and wears like leather but sews, cuts, and washes like fabric. Its papery, leathery texture softens and crinkles with handling and washing. It is very similar to the tags on the back of our Levi's! While it is super tough and not really designed for hand stitching, it is great for making bracelets, die-cutting, and serving as a base for premade appliqué patches. I highly recommend trying it out.

## Tips and Tricks for Fabric

- Unless you are using felt or leather or some other nonwoven fabric, you must take into account that the fabric will fray at the edges. In this book, if I am using a woven fabric such as quilt cotton for appliqué, I will always back it with a sew-through fusible webbing. Because it seals the back of the fabric, it allows me to cut it without worrying about fraying threads. It can also save a lot of time, as I can just iron on my appliqué piece and use decorative stitches rather than worrying about sewing it on and not covering every edge.

- If you are working with thicker fabrics, heavier floss, or items like shoes, I recommend using needle pullers. These little silicone fingertip covers will save your fingers and your sanity. Mostly I wear one on my thumb. Other times, if I need extra grip, I will also use one on my first finger. These get slippery with any oil from skin or food or hair, so keep some alcohol pads handy and wipe them off every so often.

- *Always* wash, dry, and iron any fabric you are going to use in a project with multiple fabric types to save yourself heartache at the end. There is nothing worse than spending hours making a lovely piece, washing it, and then finding the different fabrics have shrunk at different rates and your project is now lumpy. This also goes for colorfastness of thread and fabric. Most popular threads like DMC are colorfast, but hand-dyed specialty threads aren't guaranteed.

- For any leather look-alikes, use clips to hold the pieces together while stitching, not sewing pins. This fabric doesn't heal like woven cotton or linen, and pins will place unwanted permanent holes in the fabric.

## THREAD

There are many different threads that you can use in embroidery. From cotton to silk, wool, plastic tinsel, and even hair, your thread will play a significant part in the look and feel of your finished project.

### Six-Stranded Cotton Floss

The most common thread is a six-stranded cotton floss, with the most popular brands being DMC and Anchor. They come in a huge array of colors, are colorfast and inexpensive, and have a nice sheen to them. This floss can be separated into strands to give varying line weights. Many stitchers use all six strands when embroidering, and for many projects this nice, sturdy line is great. I, however, rarely use more than three because I feel a finer line comes out smoother and sleeker. My favorite stitching technique is thread sketching, and that requires fine lines, dainty curves, and the ability to get varied line thickness within the same line.

There are specialty colors among cotton floss. My favorites are variegated-color skeins (DMC and hand-dyed). The thread of these skeins changes between two to four colors. Some are very subtle, and some can get pretty crazy! When stitched, they can resemble fur, light and shadows, watercolors, and so on. You can find the DMC brand in many craft stores, but if you want some truly magnificent colors, you may need to take a trip to a local sewing shop or shop online.

## Perle Cotton

Perle cotton is a wonderful thread that
I use often because it provides a great
texture and stitches easily. It is made up
of two thicker strands twisted together
into a fine rope that you use as one
single strand. Perle cotton #5 is about
the thickness of five strands of cotton
floss. Due to its ropelike appearance, it
makes a gorgeous split or stem stitch.
When used for a satin stitch, it has a very
textured appearance. If you are going
for the flat, shiny look of satin, though,
you will want to use cotton floss or silk.

## Satin

DMC makes a line of satin thread that is very glossy and very shiny. It isn't the easiest to work with because it doesn't stick to itself, and so it doesn't maintain stitches and tension well. However, with patience and practice you can make some beautiful additions to your projects. My number one tip with this thread is to keep it slightly damp. This helps the strands stick to themselves, making stitching much easier.

## Silk

Silk is an amazing but more expensive thread option. It has beautiful shine and is super strong. A single strand of silk floss can actually be used in projects that require pulling or a higher tension than normal. Due to the nature of the silk filament, you can generally use fewer strands to achieve the same thickness as cotton floss, making the higher price tag not quite as daunting. The two brands featured in the book are Kreinik and The Thread-Gatherer. Both are amazing—Kreinik has solid colors with the normal six strands, and The ThreadGatherer has variegated and hand-dyed colors with twelve strands.

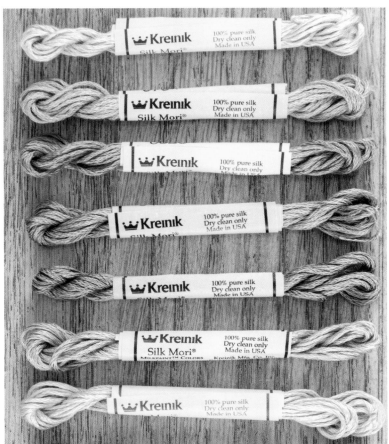

### Metallic Thread

One of the coolest effects for embroidery projects is to include metallic threads, but oh my goodness—what a pain they are to use! Most metallic threads consist of a strand of cotton floss twisted with a shiny, glittery filament. Because of this structure, they fray, twist, break, and pull. But when they behave, they look so beautiful!

## Tips and Tricks for Metallic Thread

- Use a thread conditioner like Thread Heaven or Thread Magic. You can also use your beeswax lip balm!

- Slipknot your thread to your needle. This prevents it from moving around and unraveling. To do this, take a double-length single strand and fold it in half. Put the formed loop through the eye of your needle, and put the two ends through that loop. Tighten and trim the ends to be even. Unless you are working with some incredibly tight-woven fabric, the tiny knot at the needle's eye should not interfere with stitching.

- Use a slightly bigger needle than normal with a bigger eye. This will make the hole bigger, prevent the thread from snagging, and reduce wear.

- Use shorter strands of thread than you normally would to decrease the wear on the thread.

- My favorite brand of metallic thread is Kreinik's Fine Braid. It is shiny and sparkly, but the strands are braided together rather than just twisted. This means there are less breaking and fraying issues than with others.

## Other Stitchy Crafty Supplies

### HOOPS

In many projects, an embroidery hoop will be required. Embroidery hoops keep your fabric taut, the stitches neat, and your holding hand from getting a nasty cramp. Embroidery hoops come in unfinished wood, finished wood, and plastic. They aren't expensive, and I have at least one of each size. You don't truly need one in every size though; a good 8″ hoop should work for most projects.

When working in tight spaces or on stiff fabrics like denim or shoes, an embroidery hoop is unnecessary.

Photo by Dandelyne

## SCISSORS

I recommend buying three pairs of scissors—one for cutting paper and patterns, one larger fabric-only pair, and a small pair of embroidery snips to cut threads and pick out stitches. Never use your fabric shears or your snips on paper—it's like scissors' Kryptonite!

## SEWING MACHINE

There aren't too many embroidery projects that need a sewing machine, but for pillows and stuffies it can save a lot of time. You can always hand stitch with a fine running stitch or a backstitch if you don't have a sewing machine. I also use my unthreaded sewing machine to premake holes in any kraft-tex I need to sew on.

## WASHABLE OR HEAT-SENSITIVE FABRIC MARKER

This marker will be used for freehand pattern drawings. I prefer the washable ones only because I have heard in some cases that heat-sensitive ink can return in different temperatures.

## FIBERFILL

Use this stuffing for any projects where you want a bit of fluff. There are different types—silky, firm, dry—so try them out and see what you like the best. I have no real favorite.

## VARIOUS BEADS AND BUTTONS

Beads can add a lot of dimension and sparkle to your projects. Use them instead of French knots, or replace fine stitching lines with a fine line of beads. Buttons can also add dimension and style to a simple project. Use them for eyes, flower centers, flowers themselves, and much more.

## GENERAL SEWING NOTIONS

**Ruler** *or* **tape measure**

**Straight pins**

**Wonder Clips:** These are very cool, tight-closing fabric clips that take the place of pins. They are almost a requirement when working on nonwoven materials like vegan

leather and kraft-tex, as they don't make holes. They aren't inexpensive, but if you have ever stepped on a loose straight sewing pin, they are worth their higher price!

**Iron and ironing board:** I use a mini hanging ironing board that I can drag easily all over the house.

## PAINT

**Acrylic Paint**

A few projects use some paint to decorate fabric. For washable items, you will need acrylic or fabric paint so they don't wash out.

**Watercolor Paint**

Watercolors will wash out, so only use this medium on projects that will be for decoration only.

## PRINTABLE COTTON SHEETS

If I have an image I want on my fabric, I will print the images onto printable cotton sheets. This fabric can be purchased at your local craft store and ran through an inkjet printer. Print your image out, peel off the paper backing, and stitch through it with accents, just like regular fabric. It makes a unique, quick project that looks complicated but is fast and beautiful.

# Transferring Patterns

## WASH-AWAY STITCH STABILIZER

I am an impatient stitcher. I don't want to waste even fifteen minutes tracing a pattern taped to a window onto a piece of fabric (ugh). I have sewing to do! Because of this, printable wash-away stabilizer is the only way I transfer my patterns. (I use Wash-Away Stitch Stabilizer by C&T Publishing.) Put it through your inkjet printer, peel off the backing, stick it where you want it, and stitch right through it! When you're done, get it wet and it soaks right off. It also works as a stabilizer for knit and stretchy materials, so you don't need an extra stabilizer for stitching. You can download and print any of the patterns at *tinyurl.com/11323-patterns-download*.

## Tips and Tricks with Wash-Away Stitch Stabilizer

- Press your fabric before sticking on the stabilizer. This will help it stick and keep your pattern straight.

- When doing a large project or working on fabric that moves (like linen or knits), baste the stabilizer to the fabric before starting to stitch.

- Soaking your fabric for fifteen to twenty minutes will help all the residue come off cleanly.

- When printing your pattern, use the draft setting on your printer if you are using a lighter-colored fabric. Occasionally the ink from the printer can bleed onto the base fabric if the pattern is printed too thickly. Most of the time a good soaking can get the ink out.

## DRAWING ON THE FABRIC

On lighter-colored fabrics, you can draw or trace your pattern directly onto the fabric. This is great for free-form patterns, geometric patterns, or decorative lines. There are many different markers that either wash away or disappear with heat.

## TISSUE PAPER

If you don't have a printer or you are using dark-colored fabric, tissue paper makes a great alternative. Draw your pattern onto it by tracing or drawing free-form, and then baste it or pin it to the fabric. Stitch right through it, and when you are finished, gently tear it off. Use tweezers to pick out the tissue from under satin stitches and other tightly stitched areas.

## FREEZER PAPER

Freezer paper isn't for pattern stitching but for appliqué piece cutting. Use Quilter's Freezer Paper Sheets (by C&T Publishing) to print the cut-out pattern you want. Cut out the shape with about a ¼˝ allowance; then press it onto your fabric. It will stick harmlessly, allowing you to easily cut out the pieces for your project. When you're done, simply peel it off. You can even use it again! If a project's materials list calls for two patterns—one to cut and one to stitch—this can be substituted for the paper pattern.

# Projects on Display

So you've made this really great piece of thread art ... now what? There are lots of ways to showcase your embroidery projects. Here are some of my favorites.

## HOOP IT

The easiest way to show off your work is to just leave it in the hoop you created it in! Wooden embroidery hoops come in all sorts of sizes, and the structure of the hoop makes them a snap to hang on a wall. Hoops can be wrapped with ribbon, painted, glittered, or left beautifully plain.

### Basic Instructions

**what you need**

| | |
|---|---|
| Embroidery hoop | Hot glue and glue gun |
| Completed project | Fine sandpaper |
| Scissors | (optional) |

**How You Do It**

1. Pick a hoop that is the size you need to proudly display your work. If there are any rough spots on the hoops, use the sandpaper to smooth them out.

2. Hoop the project as you want it displayed. Centering is the usual framing, but think outside the box: Would it look great offset or even cropped?

3. Gently tighten the fabric until the fabric and stitching are smooth and taut.

4. Tighten the hoop screw until very tight.

5. Trim the excess fabric to approximately ½˝.

6. Using a hot glue gun, glue the fabric to the inner hoop in small sections until the fabric is tucked under all the way around.

### Painting the Hoop

**what you need**

Use the materials in Basic Instructions (above) and add the following:

Acrylic paint (I prefer acrylic paint because it is cheap, fast drying, and easy to find. It also comes in a full rainbow of colors and is generally colorfast.)

Paintbrush

**How You Do It**

1. Use sandpaper to smooth any rough spots on the hoops.

2. Paint the outer hoop with acrylic paint. This may take 2 or more coats depending on how opaque you want the color. Use a small

fine brush to get around the metal hardware. If you get paint on the metal, use a wet wipe to clean it off before it dries.

3. After letting the paint dry *completely*, follow Basic Instructions, Steps 2–6 (page 21).

4. If you want something extra special, add painted designs to the hoop edge. Try stripes, dots, or even ombré color. This is your chance to let your creativity shine.

**note** *You only need to paint the outer hoop because you will not see the inner hoop.*

## Wrapping the Hoop

### what you need

Use the materials in Basic Instructions (page 21) and add the following:

Ribbon (½″–1″ wide)

**How You Do It**

1. Starting near the hardware of the outer hoop, secure an end of ribbon to the inside of the hoop with a dot of hot glue.

2. Wrap at a slight angle, overlapping each wrap over the previous ones.

3. Finish by gluing the end of the ribbon to the inside of the hoop.

4. Follow Basic Instructions, Steps 2–6.

## Trimming the Hoop

Use strip lace, pom-pom trim, crochet trim, or other fancy trim to run around the outside of the hoop. Painting the hoop a coordinating color will make the hoop look more finished.

### what you need

Use the materials in Basic Instructions (page 21) and add the following:

Trim: 1 piece the length of the outside of the hoop

**How You Do It**

1. Paint the hoop, if desired (see Painting the Hoop, page 21).

2. If your trim is solid, use hot glue to fix the trim around the outside of the outer hoop. If the trim is open, like lace or crochet, use a clear craft glue.

### Glittering the Hoop

Be prepared to get sparkly! As we all know, glitter gets everywhere—doing this outside will keep your house from looking like you were invaded by a herd of unicorns.

*what you need*

Use the materials in Basic Instructions (page 21) and add the following:

Fine glitter

Craft glue

Paintbrush

Acrylic sealer (*optional*)

### How You Do It

1. Paint the hoop, if desired (see Painting the Hoop, page 21).

2. Using a paintbrush, spread a layer of glue onto the outside of the outer hoop, covering about a quarter of the hoop.

3. Dump glitter onto the glue section. Tap off the excess.

4. Repeat until the entire hoop is covered with glitter. Don't forget to rinse out your paintbrush!

5. Let the glue dry completely.

6. Firmly tap off any excess glitter, and reapply glue and glitter to thin spots if needed.

7. If you want to seal the glitter, you can use a coat of clear acrylic sealer. This keeps the glitter from spreading everywhere, but it can take away some of the pure glitz of non-coated glitter.

## FRAME IT

If you don't want to use a hoop to frame your pattern, traditional framing is available. There are frame-size adhesive-backed cardboard sheets that you can use to secure your work and then fit into a purchased frame. If you have a really impressive project, you can pay a professional framer and have it last forever!

## HANG IT TAPESTRY STYLE

For Thread Sketch an Autumn Tree (page 93), I had planned on taking it to get professionally framed. In the meantime, I took two flat-head pushpins and tacked it to my wall. Time passed, and I discovered that I loved it open edged and hanging like an old-fashioned tapestry.

Here are two ways to hang a tapestry:

**Method 1:** Tack the fabric to the wall. At my favorite Japanese store, they have these neat wallhangings, and with them come clear flat-backed pushpins that are a great way to hang anything, really.

**Method 2:** Use dowels to hang the fabric like a scroll. Cut 2 dowel rods approximately ½″–1″ longer than the width of the tapestry. Fold over the top and bottom, and sew a quick line across to make 2 casings large enough for the dowels. Slide the dowels into the casings. Tie a twine to either side of the top dowel and hang on a nail. You don't need a dowel on the bottom, but it keeps the fabric straight and weighted down.

## SNUGGLE IT

If you don't want to hang your finished project, you can create some snuggly couch-worthy items from your work. After you finish your project, use coordinating fabric to make some pillows and throws.

### Throw Pillow

#### what you need

Project front

Coordinating fabric for back, in same size as front

Wonder Clips *or* sewing pins

Fiberfill

Sharp needle

Thread

Sewing machine (*optional*)

#### How You Do It

1. Clip or pin the project front and back fabric with right sides together. Sew all the way around except for a 2″–3″ opening.

2. Turn the pillow cover right sides out, and press flat.

3. Stuff the pillow to your desired firmness.

4. Close the opening with a fine whipstitch and enjoy!

For an example, look at the T. rex Stuffie (page 81) project.

### Lap Blanket

After making a throw pillow, why not add a blanket to go with it? Using appliqué techniques, sew your project to a premade blanket as a pretty accent.

#### what you need

Project front

Throw blanket

Sharp needle

Thread

#### How You Do It

1. Cut out your project, leaving a border as wide as you desire.

2. If the fabric will fray, there are a few options: Sew the project onto the blanket using a running stitch ½″ from the outside edge and allow the fabric to fray, *or* use fusible webbing to seal the fabric and iron it on. If the fabric won't fray (like felt), you can use either option with any stitch you like.

### Quilt Squares

Since many of the projects are sets, they would be perfect for using as coordinating quilt squares. C&T Publishing carries a variety of quilting books, and this would be a great reason to check them out!

# Stitch It

Beautiful things come together one stitch at a time.

—Unknown

## The Big 10

There are tons of embroidery dictionaries that list hundreds of fancy, beautiful stitches. Some are simple; some are complicated. When you pick most of them apart, however, they are just variations of what I like to call "The Big 10."

These ten stitches make up the base of so many other stitches. A star stitch, a herringbone stitch, and a long-and-short stitch are all straight stitches in different patterns. A featherstitch and a scallop stitch are just open versions of lazy daisies. Most of you should have a passing familiarity with the following base stitches, and if you don't, well, they are easy to learn!

### STRAIGHT STITCH

The straight stitch is the most basic of all stitches and is essentially the foundation for almost all other stitches. Many of the other stitches will start with a straight stitch.

1. Bring your threaded needle up through your fabric.

2. Bring your needle down through the fabric at your chosen destination depending on your pattern.

--- **Alternate Tip** ---

Using the straight stitch, you can make another very popular stitch: the *running stitch*. To do this, stitch a line of even straight stitches with spaces in between each stitch. A large widely-spaced running stitch is also called a *basting stitch*. This stitch holds two fabrics together and is removed at the end of the project. (You will see me do this to anchor my patterns in some projects.)

A *double running stitch* makes a nice outline that is the same on the front and back—great for double-sided projects! To do this, sew a running stitch along your pattern line. When you get to the end, turn around and fill in the spaces with another running stitch.

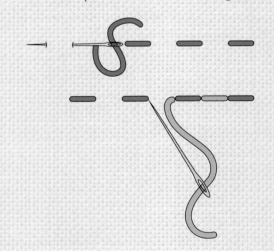

## BACKSTITCH

So useful and easy! If I could only do one stitch ever again, it would be the backstitch. Most of the projects can use this stitch as the base outline. The back of this stitch will resemble a split stitch.

1. Make a straight stitch.

2. Bring the needle up a small length to the left of your stitch.

3. Bring your needle down at the end of the first stitch.

4. Repeat Steps 2 and 3.

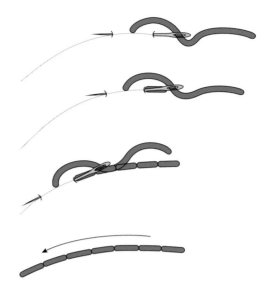

## STEM STITCH

A stem stitch is a very pretty outline stitch that looks like a rope when stitched. The back of the stem stitch looks like a backstitch. Depending on whether you keep your working thread on the top or bottom will make your "rope" twist in a different direction. Proper embroiderers will tell you that if your working thread is held up from your line it is an *outline stitch*. If it is held down, then it is a *stem stitch*. I don't have time to worry about which way the twist is going most days, so I do whichever way is comfortable!

1. Make a straight stitch, but don't pull it tight; leave a small loop.

2. Bring your needle up in the middle of the previous stitch while keeping the working thread under the line you're stitching.

3. Pull the thread to the fabric and tighten up the small loop.

4. Take the needle down past the end of the first stitch, but—again—don't pull tight and leave a loop.

5. Repeat Steps 2–4.

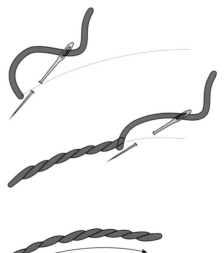

## SPLIT STITCH

The split stitch is another great outline stitch that can also be used as a fill stitch. If done properly, the split stitch should pierce the thread on top and not just separate the strands of floss. But again, who has time to worry about that?

1. Make a straight stitch.

2. Bring your needle up in the middle of that stitch, piercing the threads.

3. Go down, with the needle past the end of the straight stitch.

4. Come up, with the needle in the middle of the just-made stitch (this will be the end of the previous stitch.)

5. Repeat Steps 2–4.

--- **Alternate Tip** ---------------------------------------------

I usually work this stitch backwards, meaning that instead of coming up and piercing the thread, I like to work it like a backstitch and go down through the last stitch. This way does use more thread, but it looks the same, and it's easier to make sure you stab and split your stitch. I also find that you can use the needle to push and guide your stitches, making curves easier and tight turns cleaner.

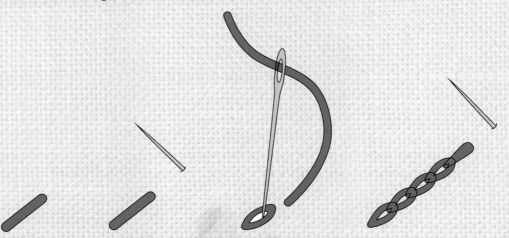

## CHAIN STITCH

This is such a useful stitch that can be altered in so many different ways to make unique looks.

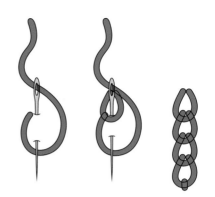

1. Bring your needle up through the fabric.

2. Go down into the same hole, but leave a loop.

3. Come up a small way down your working line. Make sure the needle is in the small loop you just made.

4. Pull the thread gently in the direction of your working line until the loop pulls taut.

5. Go down into the hole you just came up from, leaving a loop.

6. Repeat Steps 3–5, making a chain of looped stitches.

7. To finish, make a tiny straight stitch over the loop of the last stitch.

### --- Alternate Tip ----------------------------------------

This stitch can also be done backwards; in some cases, it is much faster!

1. Make a tiny straight stitch.

2. Bring the needle up a stitch length down your working line.

3. Thread the needle under the tiny straight stitch without catching the fabric underneath. (I like to use the back of the needle to do this.)

4. Go down into the stitch you just came up from to create the loop.

5. Repeat Steps 2–4, but thread under the previous loop since there will only be 1 starting straight stitch.

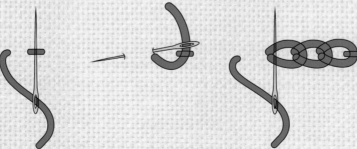

## SATIN STITCH

The satin stitch is a beautiful stitch that is just straight stitches repeated next to each other. This is used for smooth fills in smallish areas.

1. Make a straight stitch.

2. Come up right next to the top of the first stitch.

3. Go down right next to the base of the first stitch.

4. Repeat until the area is filled in.

### --- Alternate Tip ----------------

This stitch uses a ton of thread because you are basically filling the back while doing the front. You can cheat by coming up right next to the finished stitch instead of the back at the top. This leaves the stitch less of a fabric anchor, and the stitch will not be quite as puffy or smooth, but it is a good trick if you only have so much of a special thread.

Sometimes there is an area in a pattern that needs to be filled in but it is too large for a satin stitch. To fill in these larger areas, I don't get fancy; I just lay down shorter straight stitches in lightly overlapping rows until all the space is filled. I do try to focus on the direction the stitches should go. For example, if you are filling in a large space of fur, fill it in with layers of satin stitches, making sure they follow the line of the body.

## FRENCH KNOT

The French knot is my second favorite stitch! This stitch makes dots and can be used over and over to make a fill. It takes practice but is oh so worth it. Having a needle where the eye is the same thickness as the shaft is super helpful. (See Needles, page 7, for more information.)

1. Come up at the spot where you want the knot.

2. Wrap the thread around the needle 2 or 3 times (I usually do 3).

3. With the thread gently anchored so it doesn't unwrap, go down right next to where you came up. *Very important:* Leave at least a couple fabric threads in between on looser woven fabrics to keep the knot from pulling through.

4. Slowly pull the thread through while holding the top thread lightly so it doesn't tangle as it is getting pulled into the loops.

5. Repeat for another knot.

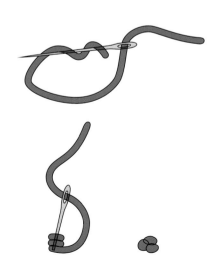

## LAZY DAISY

The lazy daisy is a single stitch from the chain stitch. Use it to make leaves, petals, fills, and decorations.

1. Bring the needle up through the fabric where you want the pointy end of the stitch.

2. Go down through that same hole, leaving a loop.

3. Bring the needle up where you want the top of the stitch to be through the small loop made by the previous step. Pull the loop taut.

4. Go down to make a tiny straight stitch that will hold the loop down to fabric.

5. Repeat to make the next stitch.

### Alternate Tip

I use versions of this stitch for so many different applications. If you alter the distance between the two end points, you can create a scallop stitch—very useful for scales and smiles. Try putting two together and make a heart. You can even place the end points in a straight line and use multiple little stitches to follow your pattern in an imitation of a couching stitch. So many possibilities just by changing the distance of the end points!

## BLANKET STITCH

The blanket stitch is a great way to make spokes, edge a blanket or piece of felt, anchor appliqué, or just make a great decoration.

**Fully on the Fabric**

1. Make a diagonal straight stitch without pulling the thread tight. Come up a space away from the base of your stitch and into the diagonal loop of thread.

2. Pull the thread taut.

3. Repeat Steps 1 and 2.

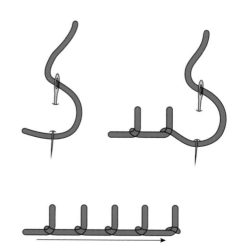

**On an Edge**

If you are working this stitch as an edging, you will work it upside down, with the spokes on the fabric and the line of thread across the seam of the two fabrics. So instead of going down and up through the fabric, the needle only goes down; then it comes up through the loop created across the top of the fabric to make a nice thread line across the edge.

If this stitch is done with each stitch right next to each other without spaces, it is called a *buttonhole stitch*!

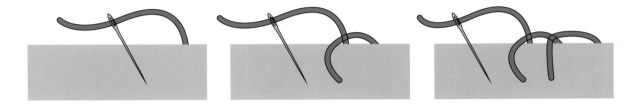

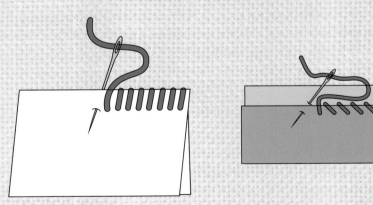

--- **Alternate Tip** --------------------------------------------------------------

A very close sibling to this stitch is the less complicated *whipstitch*. This stitch is worked the same way, but there is no threading into the loop. You just go around and around. The whipstitch is used around the edges of felt projects or when appliquéing pieces together.

## WOVEN WHEEL OR ROSE

The woven wheel or rose is a really great stitch to make dimensional flowers or fun raised circles. When weaving your thread, you can either use a tapestry needle or flip the needle over and use the eye of your needle.

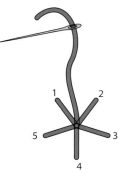

1. Using 5 (or any odd number of) straight stitches, make a spoked star.

2. Come up just outside of the middle of the star.

3. Weave your working thread under one spoke, over the next, and repeat over and under until your entire star is filled.

4. When you are done, go down with your needle just under the outer row of woven thread.

--- **Alternate Tip** ------------------------------------------------

The more strands you use, the more dimension your wheel or flower will have. Use five large green lazy daisy stitches instead of straight stitches, stop weaving before you get to the outer edge, and they look like leaves! Make multiple French knots in the center and make the five spokes evenly spaced around this cluster. Weave like normal, and you have a rose with a textured center.

# Thread Sketching

While many stitchers will use The Big 10 stitches in very specific places and ways, I have always had a very loose stitching style. I like to switch my stitches in the middle of a line or use a different amount of thread strands within the same area. I have coined this style "thread sketching." It is free-form, has no rules and no set directions, comes out beautiful, and stitches up faster than it looks!

One day while looking for a new project, I came across some of my husband's drawings. My husband is an artist and makes the most beautiful pencil and ink drawings of trees. I decided to take one of my favorites of his drawings and make it with thread. I figured that I would quickly get bored using only one color on such a detailed project, but I found that it was one of the most enjoyable projects I had ever completed. The freedom of the sketch, the beauty of the art, and the loose nature of the technique really spurred on my love of embroidery. I have included this exact project in Hang It (page 92) for you to do as well. It looks complicated, but it really isn't! Just take it slow, stitch by stitch, and it will be done before you know it.

Pencil and ink sketches get their favored appearance with loose details, tons of lines, implied subject matter, and a gorgeous marriage of thick and thin lines. Just like real ink drawings, changing the weight of your lines makes your "drawing" have depth, interest, and beauty. You can achieve this look with thread by varying the number of strands and the type of stitch used.

## CREATING DEPTH AND MOVEMENT WITH THREAD

Obviously, using more strands will make your lines thicker and using less strands will make your lines thinner. But did you know that you can get the appearance of adding a half weight by using a split stitch?

There are two different line weights achievable per strand, no matter if you use one or all six. The base thickness is just the thickness of the strands themselves stitched with a basic backstitch. Using a *split stitch* thickens the line to what I would call a half step. For example, two strands stitched in a backstitch is a size 2, whereas two strands worked in a split stitch is a size 2½. Since you can use up to six strands of floss, this will give you a total of twelve different line weights!

For many of my "sketches," I mainly use one to three strands and change my stitch type as the drawing needs. For solid areas, I will use a blended satin stitch with however many strands will fill it in fastest and cleanest. Remember, I am a lazy stitcher and won't waste time using one strand when three will cover the space faster! When filling in an area that is solid, I very rarely worry about lining up my satin stitches. I will just make any stitch that will cover the space while staying within the pattern. To blend them together, I go right through the top of the previous stitches, like a beautifully messy long-and-short satin stitch!

For nonsolid areas, I will use combinations of backstitches and split stitches. Let's say there is a line that goes from thin to thick and then back again. I will begin stitching where the line is of middling weight with two strands and a backstitch. As the line gets thicker, I will change to a split stitch. If it gets thinner again, I will go back to a backstitch and so forth until the line either gets too thin or thick for what I can achieve with two strands. If it gets finer than what's achieved with a two-stranded backstitch, I will drop to one strand and start with a split stitch as the half weight. If it gets thicker than what's achieved with a two-stranded split stitch, I will add another strand and use a backstitch. You will do the entire project following these guidelines. The reason I start with two strands and not one is I find the blending is easier and smoother when you can bury the starting points into a middle-weight stitch.

## TIPS AND TRICKS

With thread sketching, the finished project may not follow the pattern perfectly. You won't always stitch every line, or you may add a line or combine lines. This is exactly why this technique is so enjoyable—there are no rules!

Change your stitch length to get smooth lines. For tight, detailed areas, use a very fine needle and tiny stitches to get smooth curved lines. As the lines straighten out, increase the stitch length and maintain the smooth line. The finest line achievable is one strand stitched with a backstitch; the thickest (without using a satin stitch) is six strands stitched with a split stitch.

To get around little curves and very shallow bends—or just whenever a true, smooth line is needed—use an open lazy daisy or scallop stitch. Come up at the beginning part of your curve and go down at the end. Before pulling tight, bring your needle up where you need the curve. Go around the base thread and back down into the hole. Gently pull everything taut, and you should see a nice smooth curve. Sometimes you may even want to go up and around the same base thread twice at different points to make a different-shaped curve.

When doing split stitches, I always do a reverse split stitch so I can move the thread with my needle to better match the pattern. If you feel a stitch is too straight, doesn't match up right, or just needs to be nudged over, take your needle and move the stitched thread to where you need it; then go down through it to complete your stitch.

Be free. You cannot make a mistake with this technique. If you skip a half step, it won't matter. When you are finished, the result will be so sketchily beautiful you wouldn't be able to find the spot if you tried!

**The following projects use this technique:**

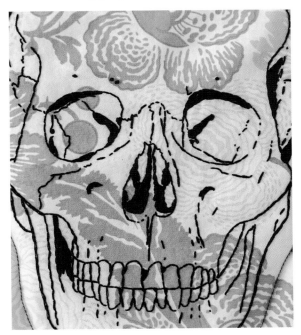

Skull Heating Pack (page 78)

Pretty Girl Handkerchiefs (page 86)

Thread Sketch an Autumn Tree (page 93)

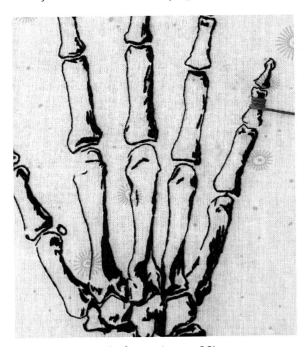

The Red Thread of Fate (page 99)

## Pile on the Glitz

I love sparklies, pretties, glitter, crystals, diamonds, rhinestones, sequins … pretty much anything that shines! I also like to add sparkle and beads to my embroidery.

### ATTACHING A SINGLE BEAD

Using a single strand, come up through the fabric just outside where you would like the bead to land. String the bead; then go back down through the fabric next to the bead. Come up where you want the next bead and repeat.

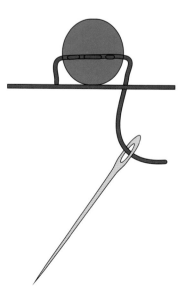

If you want the bead here…

Thread comes up and down here!

## ATTACHING A CONTINUOUS LINE OF BEADS

1. Come up through fabric at the beginning of the line. String 5 beads onto the thread.

2. Lay the beads along the stitch line, and go down through the fabric at the end of the beads.

3. Come back up underneath the last 2 beads, and put the needle back through them. These are the anchor beads.

4. To continue the line, thread another 5 beads and repeat Steps 2 and 3. To end the line, go down through the fabric at the end of the last bead.

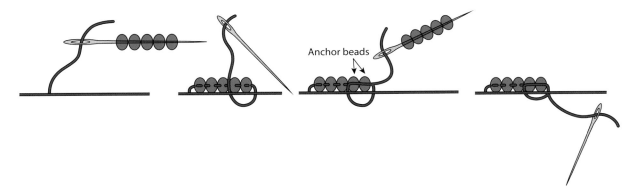

Anchor beads

## ADDING BEADS TO A STITCHED LINE

There are many ways to add beads to a path, but these two are the cleanest.

**Method 1:** Add beads to a backstitch by threading a bead onto the needle before completing each stitch. This creates a very secure beaded line.

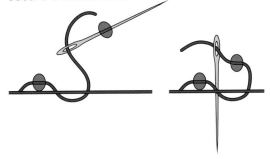

**Method 2:** If you have already stitched a line, simply use a top whipstitch and add beads that way. Bring your needle up at where the beads are to start. Thread a bead; then weave the thread under the first stitch (or sets of stitches if it is a stem or split stitch). Repeat until you reach the end of the line. Finish by going down through the fabric and tying it off. This beaded line is secure but does give the beads more movement, as they aren't anchored down one at a time like Method 1.

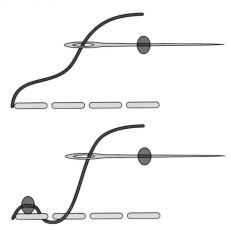

## ADDING A BEADED EDGE

To add beads around an edge, use a blanket stitch and add beads in between each stitch. (See Blanket Stitch, page 30.)

1. Come up through the fabric. Do it again in the same spot, forming a looped stitch.

2. Thread your needle through the made loop and have it exit out the top—this is how you start a blanket stitch.

3. Add a bead (or beads) onto your needle and make the next stitch like normal. The bead will want to go to the back of the project; just nudge it between your last stitch and the inside of your just-made stitch.

4. Repeat Step 3 until you reach the end of your pattern or where you started.

5. To finish a continuous edge after you have completed your last full stitch, put the needle through the bead on your starting stitch and tie off your thread with a tiny knot around the base of the starting stitch. Bury the tail on the inside of your project.

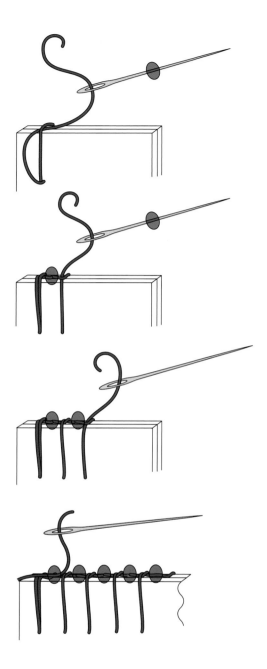

## ATTACHING A SEQUIN

1. Come up through the fabric at the center of where you want the sequin. Thread the sequin onto the needle.

2. Go down through the fabric at the outside edge of the sequin. Repeat for the next one.

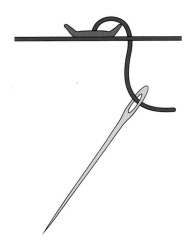

## ATTACHING A SEQUIN WITH A BEAD

1. Come up through the fabric at the center of where you want the sequin. Thread the sequin onto the needle.

2. Thread a bead larger than the center hole of the sequin; then go back down through the fabric in the center of the sequin. Repeat for the next one.

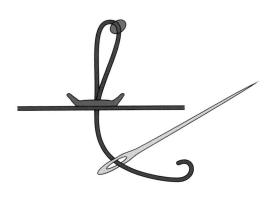

### --- Tips and Tricks

When I do a continuous line of beads, I place five at a time and anchor them down by going through the last two (see Attaching a Continuous Line of Beads, page 37). However, if the space I need to cover is smaller than five beads, I use fewer beads and only anchor through one. I have found that three is a good number to get around curves.

When attaching one bead to a specific space, don't come up through the fabric with the thread right at the spot where you want the bead. If you do, your bead will be off center. Come up right outside of the space—that way the bead will land in the middle of the space!

When attaching sequins, use contrasting thread in a star pattern for a fun look.

# THE FUN PART
## The Projects!

The part you have been waiting for!
This section is broken into three different chapters.

### WEAR IT
**42**

These patterns are (you guessed it!) on items that you wear. Here you will find shirt ideas, jewelry, and even shoes.

### USE IT
**66**

This section is dedicated to items you use all the time but that you can make more personal and interesting with some creative stitching.

### HANG IT
**92**

Here are the patterns for straight-up art. Even though it says "hang," you can also use these patterns in place of others on different projects.

# How to Use the Instructions

As a stitcher, and in general as a maker, I am loose. I don't follow patterns well, and I change colors, fabrics, and stitches in the middle of a line. I found that when doing the projects, the hardest part for me was writing the instructions and then actually following them. For over half the projects, I would finish and realize I had added a line of shadow, added some beads, or changed a color. Then I had to rewrite the instructions!

I wrote the instructions in a very basic manner and added tips and tricks after each to share what worked for me. I also included the solutions I found while using the techniques. Admittedly, I hadn't tried some of the techniques given before (like stitching on tulle in Pretty Butterflies, page 105), but I wanted to try so I could pass on helpful hints, cheats, fails, and successes to you!

## notes for working these projects

### PREPARING YOUR PATTERN

For each project, prepare and transfer your pattern any way you desire. The instructions will assume you have already done this unless otherwise stated.

### MATERIALS

Since we are doing embroidery, I'm going to assume you know you need a pattern, a base fabric, a needle, thread, and scissors. If the project does not require a special form of these materials, I am going to assume you have them all ready to go. They will not be listed in the materials.

### INSTRUCTIONS

My instructions may be looser than you are used to; this is on purpose. I want you to be creative and really get to know your needle and thread, make up your own tricks, and find new stitches and colors that speak to you. There is nothing hard-and-fast in my embroidery rule book! I have included contact information in the back of the book, so feel free to ask questions or chat about projects.

# WEAR IT

People will stare. Make it worth their while.

—Harry Winston

**43**

### Feathered Jean Skirt
*A simple jean skirt elevated by a gorgeous peacock feather*

**46**

### Winged Shoes
*Small wing designs stitched on mommy-and-me shoes*

**48**

### Collar and Cuffs
*A simple button-down dressed up with delicate flowers*

**51**

### Sweater Elbow Patches
*Pretty mushroom and flower patterns on vegan leather*

**54**

### Stacking Bracelets
*Easy, wearable leather-look bracelets*

**57**

### Heart Rhythm Workout Tank
*A workout tank accented with a sinus heart rhythm*

**59**

### Constellation Mini Hoop Necklace
*Tiny glowing constellations for necklace hoops*

**61**

### Trim a Men's Classic Shirt
*Free-form trimming for men's button-downs*

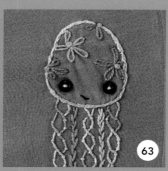

**63**

### Under the Sea Baby Clothes
*Baby items adorned with hand-stitched jellyfish and a little mer-bun*

# Feathered Jean Skirt

Peacocks shine bright with their gorgeous plumage, and so should you!
Stitch a flowing peacock feather onto a simple jean skirt and
turn it into a stunning not-so-simple fashion piece.

## what you need

Preshrunk jean skirt

Thread, floss (3 or more strands),
*or* perle cotton

Needle pullers

## How You Do It

1. Apply the pattern (page 45) to your skirt.
(See Transferring Patterns, page 19.)

2. Hoop your chosen stitch area if it is accessible.

3. Stitch the pattern using your favorite stitches.

4. Soak off the pattern paper if needed.

5. Dry your skirt and show off your work!

## Tips and Tricks

In the sample, I used variegated perle cotton in bright peacock colors. The center is done in a satin stitch, and all the feathers are a backstitch. The black outlines are lines of stem stitches lined up together. I didn't follow every line of the feathers. You can make the lines as full as you want.

If you don't have a skirt, jeans will work just as well. Try the feather on the bottom of the pant leg or on the thigh. Shrink it down and do a smaller version on your baby's jeans to match.

Jeans will be hard to hoop in many places, and denim is a hearty fabric. Patience, a solidly applied pattern, needle pullers, and a sharp, larger needle are needed.

Because jeans get washed often, be sure to use sturdy knots and tuck in the ends to finish threads.

Keep your stitch length to less than a ½˝ on the outside to avoid snagging.

# Winged Shoes

Shoes may not be the first place you think to embroider, but there is no better way to make your shoes your own. With this pattern, Hermes won't be the only one with wings on his feet!

## *what you need*

Soft canvas shoes

Thread, floss (3 strands), or perle cotton

Needle puller

## How You Do It

**1.** Apply the patterns (next page) to the sides of your shoes. Make sure to print mirror copies.

**2.** Stitch the pattern.

**3.** Wash off the pattern paper and let dry.

**4.** Show off your kicks!

## Tips and Tricks

For the samples, I used a combination of variegated perle cotton and metallic thread with backstitches and stem stitches. For the baby shoes, the inside is one strand of floss and one strand of metallic thread.

There isn't anything complicated about stitching on shoes, other than the small spaces and thick material. I used a combination of different outline stitches and regular and metallic thread.

Try this technique on baby shoes, and surprise a new mom with something no one else will have at playgroup!

Shoes can be awkward to stitch on, but sharp needles and needle pullers can be very useful. Try to finish off your threads with small knots to keep your stitching secure and your shoes comfortable.

# Collar and Cuffs

Stitch pretty little flowers on your collar and cuffs to sweeten up a classic shirt or blouse.

## How You Do It

1. Place the pattern (next page) onto the collar and cuffs of the shirt.

2. Stitch the pattern.

3. Wash, dry, and show it off!

Collar

Cuffs

## Tips and Tricks

For the sample, I used Kreinik Silk Mori Milkpaint thread to add a level of shine and lushness. I used satin stitches and stem stitches for the vines and decided to use lazy daisies for the pink flowers, but a satin stitch would also look great.

This is a very straightforward project, so try experimenting with new stitches, color stories, and image sizes. I used silk thread and lots of satin stitching for a shiny, rich look.

Keep the back of your stitching on the collar very clean, as it may be visible.

Collars and cuffs tend to be double layered, so hide the ends between the two layers of fabric.

# Sweater Elbow Patches

Elbow patches may seem old-fashioned, but they add great flair to
plain sweaters or jackets, and they protect your elbows!

## How You Do It

1. Place the pattern (page 53) firmly onto the "leather."

2. Stitch the pattern.

3. Wash off the pattern, dry the material, and cut out
the patch.

4. Using Wonder Clips or sewing pins, clip your patch
onto the elbow of the sweater.

5. Use the perle cotton to whipstitch the patch onto
the sweater.

## Tips and Tricks

I used so many different stitches on these! While most of the pieces are done in a stem stitch, I just did what I felt would look the best. I added some French knots where I felt a dot or two were needed.

There are many fabrics you can use for the patches besides leather. Try felt, scraps from another sweater, flannel, or patterned cotton fabrics. You don't even need to embroider a pattern on them if you like the simple look.

You can use double-sided fusible webbing to iron on your cloth patches rather than sewing them on. Be aware that some vegan leathers will melt, so test first!

I personally made the mistake of leaving the washable pattern paper on the leather too long (think a couple months—oops!), and I did have a little trouble getting it all off. Just keep in mind to do the project fairly soon after preparing it.

It will be easier to stitch your pattern to a larger piece of fabric and then cut out the patches.

Try using contrasting thread when stitching on your patches for an extra pop.

# Stacking Bracelets

Some kraft-tex, a simple line of stitching, and a few sparkly beads
and you have a stack of pretty bracelets ready for any outfit!

## what you need

Strips of kraft-tex (by C&T Publishing):
¼″–½″ wide × 6″ long

Perle cotton *or* floss (6 strands)

Beads: 4 per bracelet, with holes big
enough to fit 1 strand of perle cotton

Seed beads, crystals, shells, and so on

Beading needle

Pattern (*optional*)

## How You Do It

1. Use an unthreaded sewing machine to punch holes in long patterns down a piece of kraft-tex (see the sample patterns, below). Use 1 straight line, 3 straight lines, a zigzag—anything you want. I did this first before cutting out my strips.

2. Stitch into the holes in varying patterns. Try a single running stitch with a bead every stitch; go up into a hole, wrap around the strip, and go back down; make zigs and zags—this is where you get to be creative and stretch the limits of a simple line of holes! (See Pile on the Glitz, page 36, for beading ideas.)

3. Once you're done, use an 8″ piece of perle cotton and bring your needle up through the end hole halfway. Bring your needle back down through the same hole, creating a loop with the 2 ends of the thread below and of equal length. Put the 2 loose ends through the loop and tighten, creating a slipknot.

4. At the end of each hanging strand, place one of the larger beads and tie a knot below the bead so it doesn't fall off.

5. Repeat Steps 3 and 4 on the other side, and use the strands to tie the bracelet together around your wrist.

6. Wear these pretty bracelets by themselves or stack them together for a greater effect!

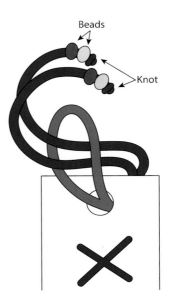

Beads

Knot

## Tips and Tricks

I used different colors of kraft-tex for my bracelets. kraft-tex is light, looks fun and leathery, and is really tough stuff!

Use different materials to see what you like the best. You can also do this with doubled-up wool felt.

Add beads to your pattern, or stitch the whole pattern in beads, even. A line of crystal beads down the middle would look amazing.

Instead of using string to tie the bracelet to your wrist, you could easily add a simple jewelry ring and clasp to connect the ends.

Combine with your other bracelets for the ultimate stack!

# Heart Rhythm Workout Tank

Spice up a plain T-shirt or tank with an easy sinus heart
rhythm, and be the envy of all your gym buddies!

## what you need

Workout tank

Wash-away stabilizer:
Approximately 2″ × 10″ for pattern

Embroidery hoop

## How You Do It

1. Place the pattern (page 58) on the workout tank,
making sure not to stretch the fabric. In this case, I
recommend using wash-away stabilizer because of
the nature of the fabric.

2. Stitch the pattern.

3. Wash away the pattern, and enjoy your new shirt!

## Tips and Tricks

For the sample, I used all six strands of a red variegated floss and a split stitch.

When sewing on stretchy knits, thread tension is key. Take your time; use even, firm tension; and the results will be smooth, with no pulling or puckering.

Make sure the fabric has been washed and dried to take care of any shrinkage before stitching.

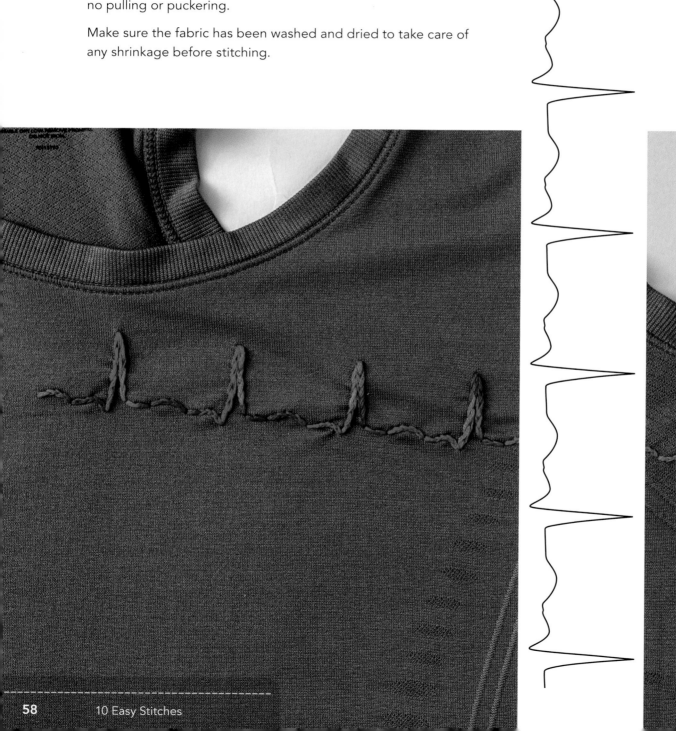

# Constellation Mini Hoop Necklace

Using mini embroidery hoops allows you to wear your beautiful
embroidery as jewelry. They come in so many fun sizes; you are sure
to find the perfect frame for your next statement piece.

## what you need

Mini embroidery hoop kit

Linen or lightweight fabric: 1 square,
approximately 2˝ larger than hoop

Embroidery hoop for stitching

Hot glue for finishing

Glow-in-the-dark thread (*optional*)

Small silver beads (*optional*)

Wash-away fabric marker (*optional*)

## How You Do It

1. With a wash-away marker or pencil, draw
2 circles on the fabric—one the size of the mini
hoop's inner circle and another ½˝ larger than
the inner circle.

2. Apply the pattern (page 60) to the fabric,
making sure it fits inside the inner circle. (The
given patterns are sized for a 1˝ hoop. If you
want them bigger or smaller, size them on a
computer or copier.)

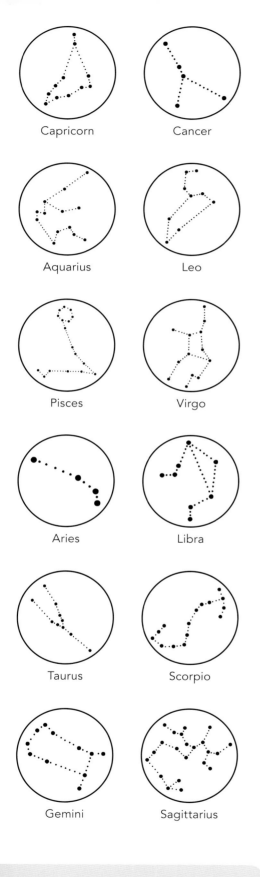

Capricorn

Cancer

Aquarius

Leo

Pisces

Virgo

Aries

Libra

Taurus

Scorpio

Gemini

Sagittarius

3. Hoop up the fabric in a regular embroidery hoop and stitch the pattern. Add the beads as the larger stars or use French knots.

4. Wash out the marker or pattern paper.

5. Cut out the stitching using the *outside* circle as your guide.

6. Follow the finishing instructions for your chosen mini hoop, as each brand may be slightly different.

7. Wear your piece with pride!

## Tips and Tricks

For the sample necklaces, I used Dandelyne hoops. (The fabric came from an old blue pillowcase!) I painted and glittered my hoops, but you can always finish them just like you would your larger hoops. In one necklace, I sized up the pattern to fit a 1½˝ hoop and used Kreinik's Glow-in-the-Dark Thread. The other is a 1˝ Dandelyne hoop with regular thread and size 15 silver seed beads.

Finishing these hoops takes some patience, but once you do it you will want to make twenty!

I find that lighter-weight fabric tends to lay nicer when finishing your hoop, but try different fabrics to decide what you like best.

My favorite brand of mini hoop is by Dandelyne. Sonia hand finishes them all and has great video tutorials. Find her on Etsy and YouTube.

# Trim a Men's Classic Shirt

Men's clothing deserves some amazing accents, too! Using simple lines and tone-on-tone palettes will keep these shirts looking masculine and sharp.

## *what you need*

Button-down shirt

Wash-away fabric marker

Embroidery hoop

Ruler

## How You Do It

1. Using your ruler, draw vertical lines onto the back of the shirt. Use the horizontal back seam as a starting place.

2. Stitch the drawn lines.

3. Wash the shirt to erase the marker lines. Dry, iron (if needed), and give it to the lucky gentleman.

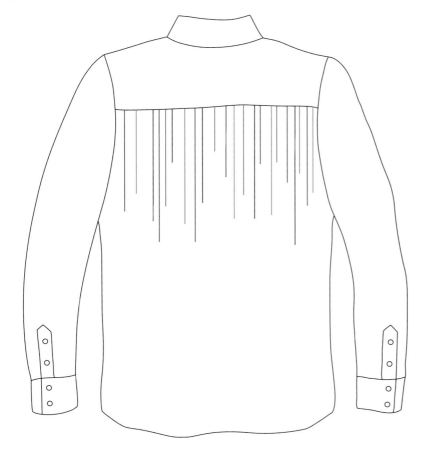

## Tips and Tricks

I had my husband put on the shirt I chose so I could measure where I would stitch. I marked each shoulder blade to make the edges even and also the middle of his back. From there, I randomly drew lines with the ruler and started stitching without any real plan. I used variegated cotton floss and a stem stitch, varying between one and six strands for the lines. I found that a single strand line looks really nice close to a thicker line. I used a design eye to judge the length and make the lines into a pleasing pattern.

I found that using a really big 12″ hoop worked great for stitching.

Don't pull the stitches too tight! Once you unhoop the shirt, the stitches will look puckered. A good steam iron worked well to get my stitches nice and smooth.

You can use pattern paper if you don't feel comfortable drawing directly on the shirt or if your shirt is a dark color.

To tie in the back and the front of the shirt, you can add lines to the front lapels, cuffs, or down just one side.

# Under the Sea Baby Clothes

Embroidery and baby clothes go together like peanut butter and chocolate. Use these sweet little sea creatures for a boy or a girl, and the mom to be will ooh and aah!

## what you need

Baby clothes (Body suits, baby pants, or receiving blankets work great!)

Embroidery hoop

Pattern

Mini black buttons for eyes (*optional*)

Fusible interfacing: 6˝ × 6˝ (*optional*)

**note** Small buttons can pose a safety hazard for babies and young children. You may wish to embroider eyes with satin stitches instead of using buttons.

## How You Do It

1. Place the pattern (below left and next page) onto the baby item, making sure not to stretch the fabric. Gently hoop the baby item.

2. Stitch the pattern.

3. Wash away the pattern and dry.

4. *Optional:* Cut interfacing ½″ bigger than the backside of the stitching. Iron on the interfacing over the back of the stitches. This makes them secure for washing and creates a smooth surface so the stitches don't scratch the baby.

## Tips and Tricks

The mer-bun was stitched in mainly a backstitch with a little satin heart. For the jellyfish, I used variegated perle cotton; I used an imitation of a couching stitch for the green tentacles. I put a tiny straight stitch over the bigger stitch to shape it where I wanted it to go.

Traditional placement for images on baby items is the center of the chest. For something different, try making your patterns offset, making them bigger, letting them wrap around to the back, or even putting them on the butt!

When sewing on stretchy knits, thread tension is key. Take your time; use even, firm tension; and the results will be smooth, with no pulling or puckering.

Make sure the fabric has been washed and dried to take care of any shrinkage before stitching.

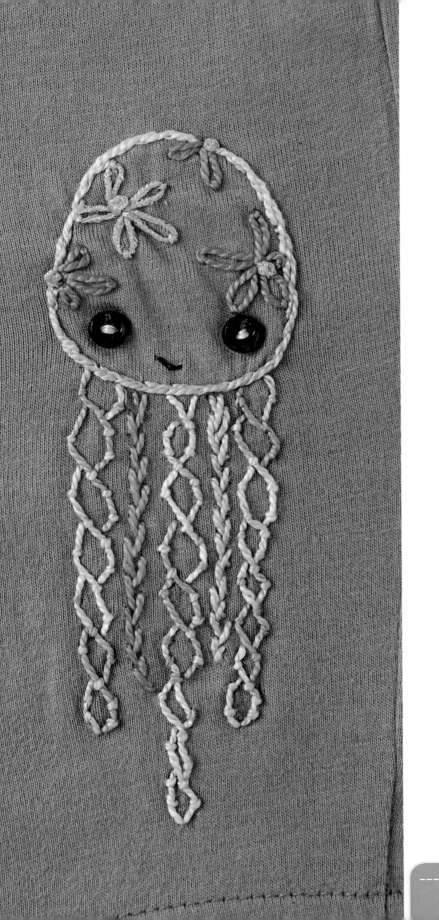

# USE IT

Have nothing in your houses that you do not know to be useful or believe to be beautiful.

—William Morris

### Beaded Christmas Ornaments
*Russian-inspired heirloom decorations*

### Rainy Day Baby Mobile
*A pretty baby mobile for the nursery*

### Painted Grocery Bag
*An upcycled, reusable grocery bag with a colorful hot-air balloon*

### Reusable Snack Bags
*Fabric snack bags featuring simple flowing embroidery*

### Skull Heating Pack
*A realistic skull pattern perfect for a rice-filled heating pack*

### T. rex Stuffie
*An awesome T. rex pillow for your favorite kiddo*

### Emperor Penguin Pincushion
*An aquarium-inspired emperor penguin and baby pincushion*

### Pretty Girl Handkerchiefs
*Thread-sketched girlish figures on dainty handkerchiefs*

### Sashiko Book Covers
*Japanese-inspired sashiko patterns adorning sturdy covers for your favorite books and journals*

# Beaded Christmas Ornaments

A Russian-inspired coordinated set of heirloom Christmas ornaments will be a passed-down treasure. Use these beaded ornaments to really stretch your beading skills! For reference on adding beads, see Pile on the Glitz (page 36).

## what you need

Felt: 2 squares 4″ × 4″ for ornament base

Felt scraps for decoration

Beads (The silver and gold beads shown are size 15 seed beads; the others are a mix of Swarovski crystal, size 11 seed beads, and various-sized sequins.)

Thread to match felt colors for beading

Thread for stitching decoration (The sample uses metallic thread.)

Patterns: 2 total—1 paper for cutting and 1 for stitching (*Optional:* Freehand or using a marker will work.)

Fiberfill

Sharp embroidery needle

Beading needle

## How You Do It

1. Use the paper patterns (pullout page P1) to cut out the pieces for the ornament.

2. Get creative and use the given patterns as starting points for your design. I suggest you choose a five-color palette and just start stitching. Use the samples as inspiration, or look online for beaded ornaments.

3. If you want to try the felt inlay, cut the section you want to use as the inlay from the stitching pattern. Stick it to the other color of felt, and cut it out. Depending on your pattern and placement, either whipstitch it to the base or use a backstitch. When you get to the edges, be slow and gentle so as not to tear the little felt piece.

4. When the front is finished, place it on the back with wrong sides together, and use a beaded blanket stitch around the edge (see Pile on the Glitz, page 36). Leave a small hole and stuff with fiberfill. Continue sewing until closed.

5. For the hanger, you can glue a string and attach a bow over it or get creative with a long length of metallic thread. I threaded the gold thread between the 2 pieces under the center bead and tied a loop. I stuffed the knot between the 2 pieces of felt and wrapped the remaining thread tightly around and around the neck of the ornament. I tied off with a knot around all the wraps in the back and buried the end into the ornament.

## Tips and Tricks

I loved making these. I used five different colors of felt and then gathered some sequins in matching colors, also adding gold and silver beads and thread. I did not have a plan for any of them other than the base patterns. I just started and kept adding until I was satisfied. I found that inlaying the other colors of felt was fun and added a really neat complexity to them. Using the same color of thread to add topstitching provided texture.

When cut into thin pieces, felt is very delicate. Handle and stitch with care if using inlays.

I would stitch as little as I needed to make the pattern work and soak off the pattern before stitching all the tiny details. The pattern paper can be difficult to get out from under inlays and satin stitches, and it can make the beading looser than you want.

# Rainy Day Baby Mobile

Sparkly raindrops, golden stars, and puffy white clouds are the perfect decoration for a little baby's nursery! This is for decoration only and *not* a toy, so be sure to hang it far above the baby's reach.

## what you need

White felt: 8″ × 8″ for clouds

Gray felt: 4″ × 4″ for raindrops and moon

Soft blue felt: 4″ × 4″ for raindrops

Yellow felt: 4″ × 4″ for stars

Iron-on silver glitter vinyl: 4″ × 4″

Iron-on metallic gold vinyl: 4″ × 4″

Wooden dowel (⅝″ diameter): 12″ long

Sparkly ribbon: About 24″ for hanging

Metallic silver thread (Kreinik metallic braid works best.)

Hot glue

Fiberfill

White thread to stitch clouds

Paper pattern for cutting out pieces

## How You Do It

1. Following the product directions, press the silver glitter sheet to the gray felt and the metallic gold sheet to the yellow felt.

2. Using the patterns (page 72), cut out all the shapes from the felt. To match the sample, you will need 8 clouds, 8 silver drops, 8 blue drops, 10 stars, and 1 moon.

3. Place 2 clouds together, and use white thread and a blanket stitch or whipstitch to stitch around the edges. Stuff with a bit of fiberfill before the last closing stitches. Do this for all the clouds, and you will end up with 4.

4. For the silver raindrops, place the non-glitter sides together. Using the silver thread, tie a knot in one end. Bring the thread up through only one layer at the bottom (this hides the knot) and do a straight running stitch through both layers to the top. When at the top, only go through one layer from outside to inside. Bring that thread up so that the raindrop is hanging off the end. This thread will now be the attachment thread for the dowel, so cut it at the hanging length.

5. For the blue raindrops, start at the top of each drop and use a running stitch around the edge with the silver thread. When back at the top, only go through one layer from outside to inside. Bring that thread up so that the raindrop is hanging off the end. This thread will now be the attachment thread for the dowel, so cut it at the hanging length. I used about 11″ for mine because I adjusted them for different lengths when assembling.

6. Use a piece of sandpaper to remove any rough spots or splinters on the wooden dowel. In a pinch, you can use a paper grocery bag for minor smoothing. If you want, paint the dowel and let it dry completely. I didn't paint my dowel, but I did glitter it!

7. The dangling pieces are each made of 1 cloud, 1 silver drop, and 1 blue drop. Thread 1 raindrop thread onto a needle and thread through one side of the cloud. Do the same with the other raindrop thread. Assemble 4 total dangling pieces.

8. Lay out the 4 sets how you want them to dangle, making some raindrop threads shorter and staggering them to look pretty. The cloud is loose and can be adjusted up and down the 2 raindrop threads. Place the dowel across the threads. When you have them all at the lengths you want, trim the threads at the top of the dowel. If you need to, place a tiny mark where the threads will be on the dowel.

9. Use a drop of hot glue to attach each end of the threads to the back of the dowel.

10. Glue the ends of your hanging ribbon to make a loop big enough to fit the end of the dowel. Place the dowel into the loops, and secure in place with a drop of hot glue on the inside.

11. Hang up the mobile and adjust the clouds. Decide where to place the stars and moon. Make a sandwich with them and the thread they will hang from by hot gluing them together with a small dot in the center. I put 1 star on each set, 2 single ones on the dowel, and the moon on the hanging ribbon.

12. Hang your mobile somewhere special and enjoy!

## Tips and Tricks

You don't need to use the iron-on silver glitter or metallic gold vinyl. This pattern will look very cute with plain felt and metallic threads. If you want to add accents, try adding sequins or beads instead.

Before inserting the thread through the clouds, string a bead above each raindrop.

If you are a die-cut fan like me, you may have similar cloud, raindrop, and star shapes in your stash. Feel free to use them and save some cutting time!

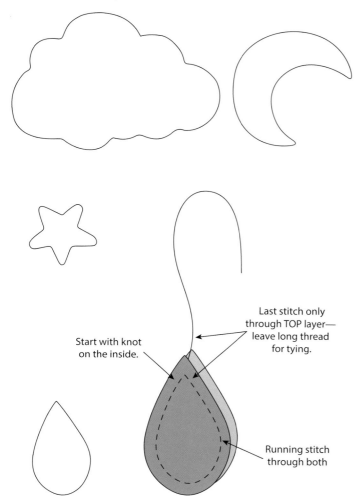

Start with knot on the inside.

Last stitch only through TOP layer—leave long thread for tying.

Running stitch through both

Make 4 sets and vary the lengths.

# Painted Grocery Bag

Don't suffer with boring, plain grocery bags—upcycle them! Use a plain cloth bag, some paint, and a bit of creativity to alleviate your grocery doldrums.

## what you need

Plain fabric grocery bag

White felt for clouds

Fiberfill

Patterns: 2 total—1 on wash-away pattern stabilizer for stitching and 1 on paper to trace pattern onto bag

Wash-away fabric marker

Acrylic paint and paintbrush

Embroidery hoop (*optional*)

## How You Do It

1. Print or trace and then cut out the entire hot-air balloon (pullout page P1) onto the bag using the washable marker.

2. One by one, cut off sections of the pattern along the pattern lines. Trace each edge onto the bag as it gets cut off. I cut the bigger portions and not every line. Decide the colors and pattern you want before cutting.

3. Paint the hot-air balloon using acrylic paint. Get creative; be bright! Let the paint dry completely.

4. Once the paint is dry, apply the stitching pattern over the paint. The pattern may not match perfectly due to tracing and painting differences, so apply it as best as possible.

5. Stitch the pattern right over the paint. If the paint doesn't match the pattern lines, follow the paint! This will keep the stitching nice and lined up when you wash off the pattern.

6. Wash away the pattern and let the bag dry completely. The acrylic paint won't wash off.

7. Cut out clouds from white felt. Use a whipstitch to secure the clouds onto the bag. Before finishing the stitching, stuff with a bit of fiberfill to make them puffy. To make it appear that the clouds are behind the balloon, just trim off the part of the cloud that wouldn't show and stitch in place.

8. Take your bag shopping!

## Tips and Tricks

For my bag, I used a chain stitch for the outline and the inside section dividers. To give the illusion of dimension, I used black thread on the outside sections, charcoal thread on the next couple of sections inside, and then medium gray on the middle sections.

For the chevrons, I used gold and silver thread and a satin stitch. The bottom of the balloon is made up of gold and silver rows of chain stitches. The tiny patriotic bunting on the basket is red, white, and blue split stitches. To tie the handle into the rest of the bag, I ran a running stitch through it in gold thread.

Instead of paint, you could use appliqué techniques and colorful fabrics.

You don't need a stitching pattern if you would rather just follow the lines of your painting.

Instead of white felt, try fake white fur for a fun tactile addition.

Add glitter paint, beads, sequins, and anything that you feel would make your bag yours!

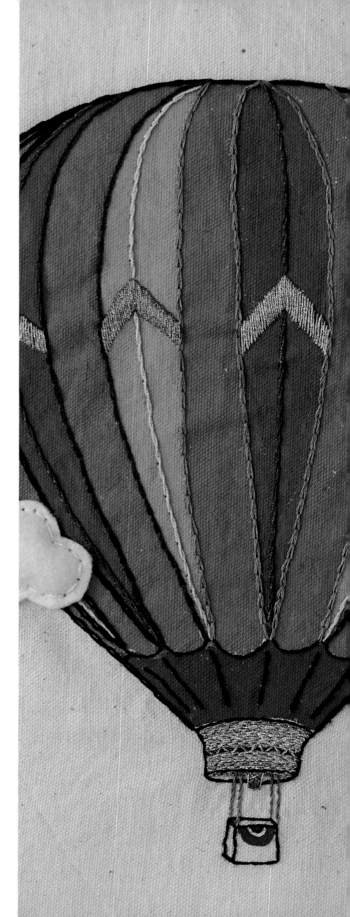

# Reusable Snack Bags

Some cotton, water-resistant fabric, fusible webbing, and a simple flowing pattern make for really fun (and environmentally friendly!) snack baggies.

## what you need

Fabric: 1 piece
6¾″ × 15¾″ for top

Water-resistant
fabric: 1 piece
6¾″ × 15¾″ for inside

Fusible webbing:
1 piece 6¾″ × 15¾″

Sticky-back hook-
and-loop fastener:
1 strip ½″ × 6″

Pattern

Thread

Sharp needle

Hot glue

## How You Do It

1. The measurements given will make a closed bag approximately 6½″ × 7″ with a 2″ flap. From the top of the outside fabric, measure down 6¼″. This will be where you place the bottom of the pattern (pullout page P2).

2. Stitch the pattern and then wash it off. Let it dry completely. Gently press from the back if needed.

10 Easy Stitches

3. Apply the piece of fusible webbing to the entire back of the front fabric, right over the stitching.

4. Peel off the webbing backing paper and lay the water-resistant fabric, cloth side out, on top. Use a cover cloth and press the 2 pieces of fabric together. The end result will be 1 big solid piece of fabric with stitching on the front and the cloth side of the water-resistant fabric on the back. It will have the feeling of a very thin wet suit!

5. Fold the fabric where the stitching ends— 6¼˝ from the end—and press in the crease. At the top of the back, fold the fabric down ½˝ and press. Fold the top flap down just to the top of the stitching (this should make the top flap about 2˝), and press that crease.

6. After all the pressing is finished, the bag should have taken its final shape. If there are any errant edges, trim with scissors or a rotary cutter to make them even. It's okay to cut through a tiny bit of stitching, as the stitches have been sealed with the fusible webbing.

7. Using a line of hot glue within the ¼˝ seam allowance, carefully glue the edges of just the bag section together. You can also sew the edges together, but I wanted this bag to be able to hold water. (Sewing requires making holes!) Also glue the ½˝ folded edge at the top of the flap.

8. Apply the whole (both sides together) hook-and-loop strip to the ½˝ edge at the top of the flap. Peel off the backing to the open side, and carefully fold over and stick it just above the stitching.

9. All done! Use for snacks, sandwiches, and everything in between. Because it has a water-resistant fabric lining, it can hold juicy fruits and snacks without getting messy!

## Tips and Tricks

For the stitching, I used a simple backstitch and altered the number of strands to create different line weights.

The water-resistant fabric I used is the lining fabric for baby diapers! This is easy to find at any major fabric store or online.

Alter the fabric size to easily change the baggie size.

Get rid of the flap altogether and place the hook-and-loop strip on the top inside edge.

To make these faster to produce, skip the embroidery and use cool fabric.

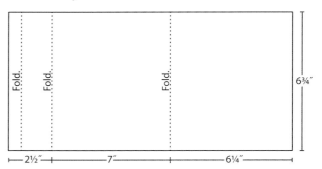

# Skull Heating Pack

What better image to have on a heating pack than the awesome human skull? This large rice-filled heating pack is perfect for when you're feeling under the weather.

## what you need

Fabric: 12˝ × 15˝ for front

Coordinating fabric: 12˝ × 15˝ for back

Uncooked rice: About 2¼ pounds or 4½ cups

Cotton thread

Washable fabric marker

Sewing machine

Funnel (optional)

## How You Do It

1. Apply the pattern (pullout page P2) to the front fabric. Because this pattern is a bit larger, I chose to do a basting stitch around my pattern to keep it from shifting.

2. Stitch the skull pattern. Use thread-sketching techniques (page 33) and 6 strands of floss for the outline and solid fill. A stem or split stitch will look best for the outline. Use 2–3 strands for the inside details. Use French knots as needed for dots or small dashes.

3. Wash away the pattern and let dry.

4. Place the back fabric right sides together with the stitched front. Use your sewing machine to sew together with a ½″ seam allowance, leaving a 3″ opening at the bottom for turning. Clip the corners and turn right side out. Use a pencil or knitting needle to poke out the corners, and press from the back so you don't smash your stitches.

5. Topstitch ½″ around the outside edge, skipping the 3″ opening at the bottom. Use the washable marker to draw a line 1″ outside the skull stitching. Topstitch on this line, leaving an 1″-wide opening right above the first turning opening. This creates an inside pocket to keep the rice better distributed. Leave long tails so you can tuck in the ends with a needle.

6. Using uncooked rice and a funnel, fill the inside pocket with rice. Don't overfill—you want enough to make it a loose 1″ thick when lying flat.

7. Carefully use your sewing machine to close the inside pocket, lining up the stitching with the previous top stitch. Alternatively, you can also use a single strand and hand stitch it closed with a tiny double running stitch.

8. Use the funnel to fill the outside rim pocket, making it even with the inside pocket. Do not overfill the corners because they will get too hot.

9. Use your sewing machine or needle and thread to close the outside hole.

10. To heat, microwave for 1–2 minutes. Always use the lower time first so the heating pack doesn't get too hot.

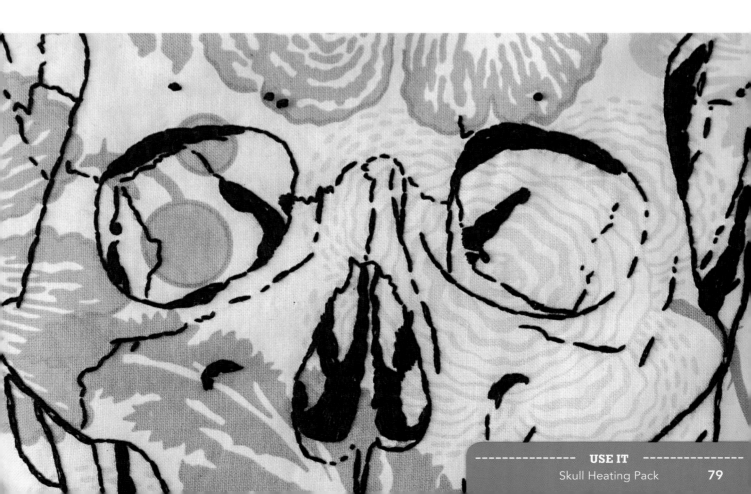

## Tips and Tricks

Add some dried lavender or a couple drops of essential oil to the rice to provide some aromatherapy.

Other fill options include flaxseed and feed corn. I really like feed corn; it moves freely, holds heat very well, and also releases moisture for an even better therapeutic effect. Just a heads-up, though—the corn does have a very corny smell that may not be ideal if you or your recipient are sensitive to scents. If you choose the corn, you may want to skip the inside pocket because the corn may be too large to fill the corners properly.

These can be made smaller by shrinking the pattern and not making an inside pocket.

Since the sewing machine will already be out, try making some hand pods by sewing simple squares of leftover matching fabric. Keep the hand pods together with the heating pack for a great gift, but drop the microwave time down to 30 seconds.

*Important:* Do not use sparkly fabric, metallic thread, beads, sequins, or fabric with metallic accents. These will be going into a microwave and getting hot, so everything needs to be cotton or heat safe.

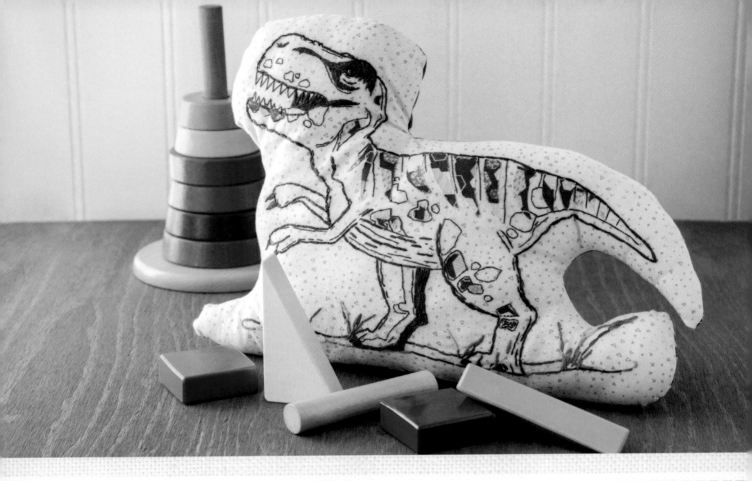

# T. rex Stuffie

All little ones love soft things, and what's better than a stuffed
dinosaur that can also be a little travel pillow?

## what you need

Light-colored fabric: 12″ × 14″ for front

Coordinating fabric: 12″ × 14″ for back

Fiberfill

Wash-away fabric marker

Sewing machine

Safety doll eye (*optional*)

## How You Do It

1. Apply the pattern (pullout page P1) to the light
fabric. Because this pattern is larger, I chose to do
a basting stitch around my pattern to keep it from
shifting.

2. Stitch the T. rex pattern. Use thread-sketching
techniques (page 33) and 6 strands of floss for the
outline and solid fill. A stem or split stitch will look
best for the outline. Use 2–3 strands for the inside
details. Add the safety doll eye or use a satin stitch.

3. Wash away the pattern. Dry and press your pillow front from the back so you don't smash your stitches.

4. Use a fabric marker to draw a line about 2″ all the way around the dinosaur. This will be the edge of your pillow, so it should be a general shape and does not need to be too detailed.

5. Cut out the front of the project along the drawn line.

6. Time to make the back! Wrong sides together, trace the outline of the stuffie shape onto the back fabric. Cut it out.

7. With right sides together, use a sewing machine to sew most of the way around, leaving a 3″–4″ opening for turning and stuffing.

8. Turn the project right side out and stuff until it is nice and puffy.

9. Close your hole with little running stitches, keeping close to the seam.

10. Give the stuffie to your kiddo, and watch their eyes light up when they see their new pillow friend!

## Tips and Tricks

In the sample, I used a variegated thread in brown, navy, and hunter green. The fabric is from Riley Blake Designs.

I used some coordinating fabric scraps to fill in some of the stripes and accents on the dinosaur. To do this, I first backed the scraps with fusible webbing. I then cut them out to fit inside the stitched stripes and carefully ironed them in place. This is completely optional and can be replaced with a satin stitch or a fun stitched fill.

Use these instructions for any pattern you choose to make different pillow friends. Try enlarging the mer-bun (page 64) for a sweet feminine version.

Use plush fabric (such as minky) on the back for a soft, cuddly finish.

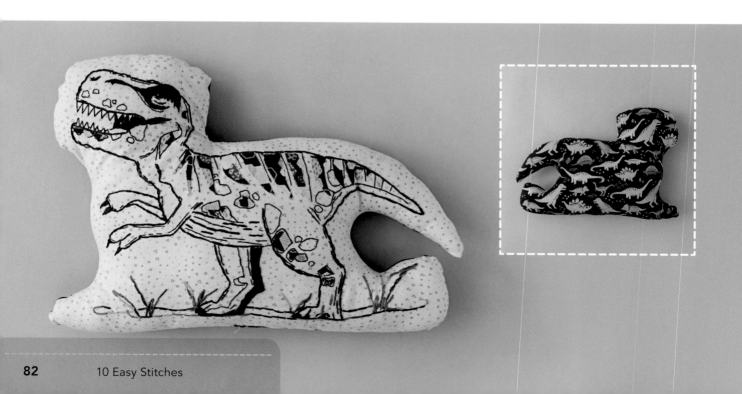

# Emperor Penguin Pincushion

Every stitcher needs a good pincushion. Make a sweet penguin pin holder to brighten up your worktable! The pattern is courtesy of the lovely Angele Carter of the FabricAndInk shop.

## what you need

Light blue felt: 4″ × 4″

Yellow felt: 4″ × 4″

Medium gray felt: 1¼″ × 11″ strip for side band, plus ¾″ × 1″

Felt scraps: White 1½″ × 4″, black 2″ × 4″, and pale gray 1¼″ × 2″

Fiberfill

Pattern: 2 total—1 paper pattern for felt pieces, 1 wash-away pattern for stitching (*optional*)

## How You Do It

1. See the patterns (pullout page P1). For the papa penguin, place and stitch the white tummy using a backstitch onto the blue base circle. Add the back piece and the beak. Add the wing on top according to the pattern.

2. Stitch the details according to the pattern. Make the yellow markings under papa penguin's chin by using different shades of orange and yellow in small straight stitches of different lengths to fill in the space and create a graduated appearance.

3. For the baby penguin, position the body and backstitch the white head in place. Use a satin stitch to stitch the black section of the head and beak. Using a light gray thread (variegated looks great here!), stitch random straight stitches over the little body to create "fluff." Backstitch the wing onto the body.

4. For the side band, apply and stitch the pattern.

5. Put together the pieces. Starting at around the 10 o'clock position, whipstitch the top to the side band using matching blue thread by holding the strip perpendicular to the top circle. This takes a bit of practice, but you'll get the hang of it!

6. Once you have sewn all the way around, there will be a small overlap of the side strip. Pin the side band seam together, and stitch the bottom to the side band starting from the seam. The overlapping part of the sideband area is where you will stuff the pincushion. Before you close the bottom, stuff firmly with fiberfill.

7. Keep stitching until you get to the overlap. Stop. There should be about 1″ without stitching. Close the bottom gap and then close the sideband.

## Tips and Tricks

For my pincushion, I used a variegated ocean color for the waves and a white metallic thread for the top wave on the side band. I used three different shades of gray for the fish. For the papa penguin, I used about four different shades of yellow and orange for his head and added a white line behind his wing to make it more noticeable. For the baby penguin, I used three different colors of gray and just kept adding straight stitches until I was satisfied with the result. I felt the bottom needed a little grounding, so I freehanded a ground with different colors of beige and gray. This part is totally optional.

The 3D part of the sewing can be a little tricky, but go slow and it will form. It is easier to stitch while holding it in its final position than trying to do it flat.

Angele created this pattern specifically for this book after she was inspired by the penguins at the Monterey Bay Aquarium.

# Pretty Girl Handkerchiefs

Using my absolutely favorite technique of thread sketching, stitch pretty girls on dainty white handkerchiefs for the perfect old-fashioned gift. Refer to Thread Sketching (page 33).

## what you need

Handkerchiefs, with or without edging

Black thread for sketch

Embroidery hoop

Colored thread for details (*optional*)

Single-sided lightweight fusible interfacing (*optional*)

## How You Do It

1. Apply the pattern (pullout page P1) to a corner of the handkerchief.

2. Hoop your stitch area.

3. Stitch the pattern using combinations of 1–2 strands of black thread according to the thread-sketching technique instructions. Because handkerchiefs are white and generally very thin, you must be careful about what the

back of your piece looks like. Take extra effort to avoid trailing your threads. If you need to move to another place of your pattern, either tie off and start again or thread under existing stitches to get where you need to be.

4. Stitch flower details in color if desired. I used Kreinik Silk Mori Milkpaint thread for a rich look.

5. Soak off the pattern paper. Because the hand-kerchiefs are so delicate, leave them in warm water for 20–30 minutes so as not to damage the stitching.

6. Since the back will be exposed, there are a couple options if you want to cover your stitches. The first is to cut a piece of single-sided fusible interfacing to just cover the back stitches. Place the handkerchief, stitches down, onto a towel and iron on the interfacing. A second option is to sew a second handkerchief to the back. The ones I used were very thin, with a pretty crochet edging around the outside. I put them together and ran a coordinating running stitch through the 2 edges.

## Tips and Tricks

For this project, all the lines are thin but they do vary in weight. I used one to two strands throughout and changed my stitch type based on the drawing. With thread sketching, the finished project may not follow the pattern perfectly. You won't always stitch every line, or you may add a line here and there. Sketches are free-form, and so should your stitching be.

# Sashiko Book Covers

Remember when we used paper bags to cover our books? Using kraft-tex, this is the grown-up version of the old-school book cover! kraft-tex is too hard to hand stitch by itself, but it takes appliqué like a charm!

*Sashiko* is a form of Japanese embroidery that uses a running stitch to create a pattern. Many of these patterns are geometric, but some include Japanese flowers, simplified water, and even koi fish. The Japanese word *sashiko* means "little stabs" and refers to the small stitches used in this type of embroidery.

## what you need

Book *or* journal

kraft-tex (by C&T Publishing):
1 piece sized according to the
measurements in instructions

Fabric to stitch flower appliqués
(approximately 4″ × 7″ pieces of 4 fabrics)

Fusible webbing

Sewing machine

## How You Do It

1. Measure your book. You will use these measurements to cut your kraft-tex. The sample pattern is based on a composition notebook 7½″ × 9¾″.

2. Cut the piece of kraft-tex the height of the book *plus* ¼″–½″ and the length of your open book *plus* 4½″. For example, for my spineless composition book with a thin card stock cover, I needed a fabric piece 10″ × 19½″. Let's say your book is 6″ × 9″ with a 1″ spine and a thick, hard cover. In this case, your fabric will be 9½″ × 17½″ (height + ½″ is 9″ + ½″, and full length—including the spine—is 6″ + 6″ + 1″ + 4½″).

3. On the inside of the cover, mark off 2¼″ on each end. These will be folded in to create the cover flaps.

4. Make the patches. Cut apart the pattern (pullout page P2) into separate flowers and apply the patterns to the fabric. I used 4 different fabrics and stitched one of each flower size onto each fabric.

5. Stitch the patterns, wash off the pattern paper, and let it dry completely.

6. Apply fusible webbing to the back of your fabric pieces.

7. Cut out the flowers and arrange them on the front and back of the kraft-tex cover. Press them in place. You can add interest by having the flowers wrap around the spine or the edges—when the cover is completed, the flowers will be on the inside panels as well as the front.

8. Make the book-cover pockets by folding the ends in at the line drawn in Step 3. Press in place. With the ends folded in, put your book inside before sewing to make sure it fits and adjust if needed.

9. Remove the book. Using a sewing machine, either sew across the top and bottom with an ⅛″ seam or use an unthreaded sewing machine to punch the holes and then use a fun coordinating thread and a blanket stitch.

10. Place your book inside its new home!

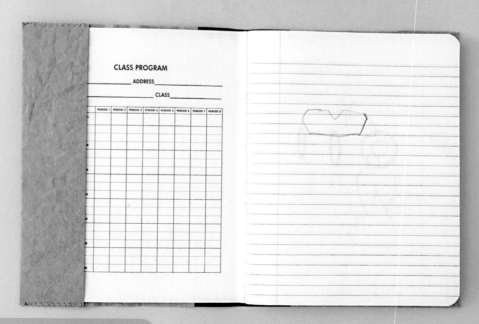

## Tips and Tricks

kraft-tex fresh out of the package is very smooth and doesn't have a leather texture. I wanted to prepare my pieces, so I crumpled them into super tight balls and then boiled them (yup—on the stove in a big pot) for ten minutes. They will flatten out in the water, and when they dry they have a great leather-like appearance.

For my cover, I really wanted to use the gray kraft-tex, but I only had 8½″ × 11″ pieces. Making a larger piece required for the cover I sewed to have a black strip in the middle, creating a spine effect. I attached the two by overlapping them ½″ and using my sewing machine to stitch them together. I did two lines of stitching for a more finished look.

When stitching the edges, I wanted to use metallic gold thread. Since hand sewing kraft-tex is so difficult, I used an unthreaded sewing machine to punch the holes into the cover and then hand stitched the flaps closed using a blanket stitch. It came out just how I envisioned it!

*Important:* Measure your book exactly. *6″ × 9″ books may not be exactly 6″ × 9″; my first sample book was actually 9⅛″.* This tiny difference made it so I couldn't stitch the flaps! Make the margins slightly bigger if you are unsure; you can always trim.

Traditional *sashiko* is done on navy-blue fabric with bright white thread. The stitches are a form of running stitch, but instead of each stitch being equal to the gap, the stitches will be double the length of the gaps in *sashiko*.

Add text to your book cover with a title, a quote, or even "Mine." Place the cut-out flower pattern pieces around the text in a pleasing design.

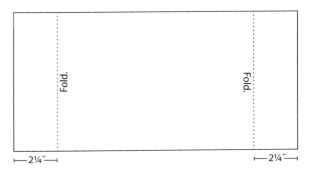

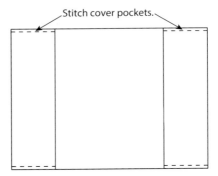

Stitch cover pockets.

# HANG IT

**Thread Sketch
an Autumn Tree**
*A dramatic sketch
recreated in thread*

93

**Immortalize
a Hand Drawing**
*A drawing translated to thread
(great for first drawings!)*

95

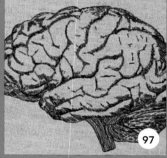

**Gray's (Not Grey's!)
Anatomy in Blackwork**
*Thread sketching a classic
anatomy woodcut image*

97

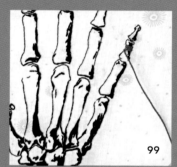

**The Red Thread of Fate**
*Stitched skeleton hands connected
by the fabled Red Thread of Fate*

99

**Woodland Animals
Nursery Art**
*Appliquéd woodland animals
ready for a nursery*

102

**Pretty Butterflies**
*Silken butterflies floating
on dainty tulle bases*

105

**Mandala Dream Catcher**
*A whimsical translation
of a traditional Native American
dream catcher*

107

**Polar Bear, Snowflakes,
and Glass**
*A wintry scene sparkling
with vintage glass beads*

109

# Thread Sketch an Autumn Tree

This tree was my first delve into thread sketching. Originally an
experiment, this is one of my favorite projects I have ever made.
The original drawing is by my artist husband, Daniel Presedo.

## what you need

Black thread

Linen or other heavier base fabric:
12″ × 16″

Printed pattern on wash-away stabilizer
(This is too complicated to trace.)

## How You Do It

1. Print or copy the pattern (pullout page P1)
and apply it to the fabric. I highly recommend
running a basting stitch around the outside.

2. Using thread-sketching techniques to stitch
the drawing.

3. Wash off the pattern and let dry completely. Gently press from the back if needed. Trim to the desired size.

4. Because of its rectangular shape, this project looks best if hung tapestry style (page 23) or framed.

## Tips and Tricks

In my sample, I used black satin thread for the entire tree. My base fabric is a cream linen. I finished my sample with a double-dowel tapestry method, using a sewing machine to make the casings in the top and bottom for the dowels. I then used a doubled-up piece of gold thread and made a quick hanger by looping the ends over the ends of the top dowel.

This is a very straightforward project. Once you get the hang of the thread sketching, the rhythm is so relaxing.

Because of the light-colored fabric and black thread, be mindful of thread trails across the back. They will show! In some places you really can't avoid it, but try for a professional look.

Finished size 10¾″ × 12¾″

# Immortalize a Hand Drawing

Copy a favorite drawing onto fabric and make it textile art with some creative thread sketching. This is perfect for children's drawings and grandparent gifts!

## what you need

Drawing

Camera *or* scanner

Fabric and thread of your choice

Hoop in size to frame your drawing

## How You Do It

1. Take a picture of the drawing with a camera in a well-lit area, or scan the drawing.

2. Print the drawing onto washable pattern paper.

3. Stitch the pattern with basic stitches or use thread-sketch techniques if the drawing warrants it.

4. Wash off the pattern and finish it off using a technique in Hoop It (page 21).

## Tips and Tricks

In my sample, I got my artwork (at right) from a great artist named Marlow, age three. The title is *My Grandpa, Grandma, and Me on a Hike*. I chose the background because it was a cute outdoor pattern, and I tried to stitch it as exact as possible to capture the drawing.

This is a very straightforward project; try experimenting with new stitches, colors, and even appliqué techniques.

Use the finished project to make a pillow front or make multiple drawings and use them as quilt squares.

If you don't have a way to create a digital copy of the drawing, you can use a washable fabric marker to trace the image onto the fabric.

This project was created to take children's drawings and stitch them as lovely keepsakes. These make amazing gifts to grandparents or to mommy and daddy.

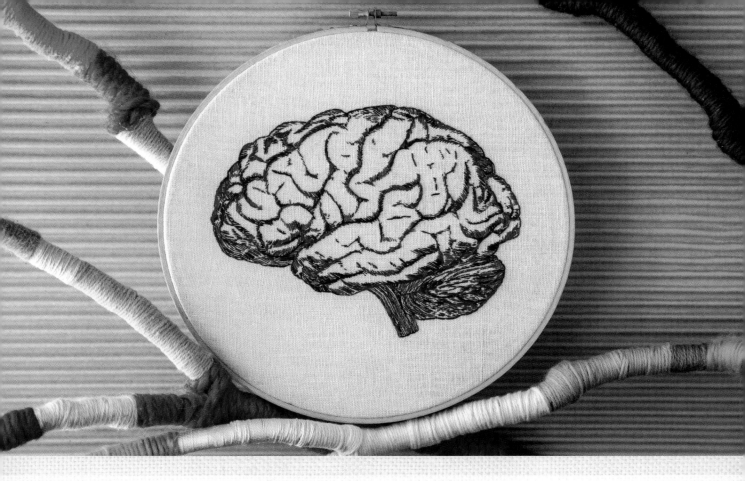

# Gray's (Not Grey's!) Anatomy in Blackwork

Henry Carter, illustrator of the original *Gray's Anatomy* text from the 1800s, created amazingly detailed drawings on wood blocks that were then engraved and used as a large printing block. Using the thread-sketching techniques (page 33), recreate these intricate drawings with needle and thread.

## what you need

- Base fabric (Linen was used in sample.)
- Variegated embroidery floss
- 9˝ wooden hoop

## How You Do It

1. Apply the pattern (page 98) to the fabric, and run a basting stitch around the edge.

2. Hoop your stitch area.

3. Stitch the pattern using combinations of 1–3 strands (mostly 1).

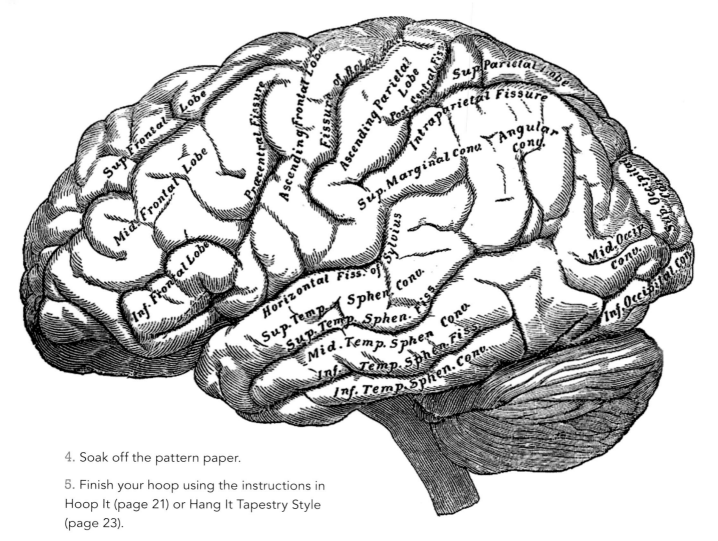

4. Soak off the pattern paper.

5. Finish your hoop using the instructions in Hoop It (page 21) or Hang It Tapestry Style (page 23).

## Tips and Tricks

For my sample, I used a variegated thread and finished it off very simply in an unpainted wooden hoop.

While true blackwork patterns are done in intricate patterns on a grid, the slashed lines of the shading in the old engravings emulate the idea without being rigid. Enjoy the detail and the zen feeling that comes with making the little hash lines, and before you know it, you will be finished!

Traditional blackwork is done in, well, black, but using a variegated floss gives a fun twist to the thread drawing.

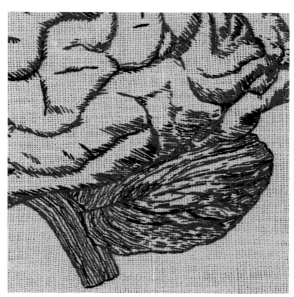

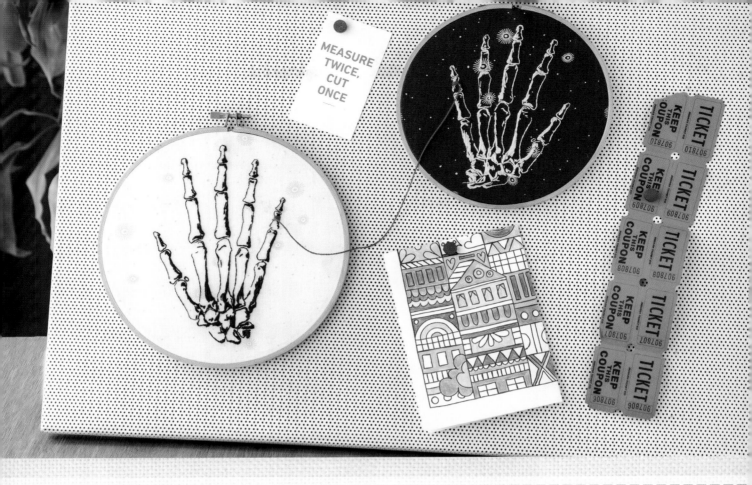

# The Red Thread of Fate

In many Asian cultures, it is believed that the gods connect two people destined to be lovers with a red string tied around the pinkies. This magical cord may stretch or tangle but will never break. This belief is similar to the Western concept of a soul mate.

## what you need

Base fabric: 2 pieces large enough to fit into 1 wooden 8″ hoop and 1 wooden 6″ hoop

8″ wooden hoop

6″ wooden hoop

Red perle cotton: 12″ length

## How You Do It

1. Apply the patterns (page 101) to each piece of base fabric.

2. Stitch the pattern using the thread-sketching technique (page 33). The patterns provided are detailed, but this is just a guideline. Do just the outsides or do every line, or decide on somewhere in the middle. This is a creative choice.

3. Hoop each hand in their respective frames and finish them as you choose. (See Hoop It, page 21.)

4. Tie a knot at the end of the red cord, and bring the needle and thread up at the pinkie of the larger hand. Sew 3 straight stitches across the pinkie of the hand to look like the string is wrapped around the finger. Let the string hang loose out of the front.

5. Leaving enough string loose to span the desired distance between the hoops, repeat this process across the pinkie of the smaller hand. Finish in the back and tie off.

6. Hang the hoops where desired.

## Tips and Tricks

For the sample, I chose two matching but opposite base fabrics that had a faint space-type look. I also used white thread on the navy fabric and navy thread with the white fabric.

Instead of perle cotton, you could use metallic red thread or even a single strand of red seed beads.

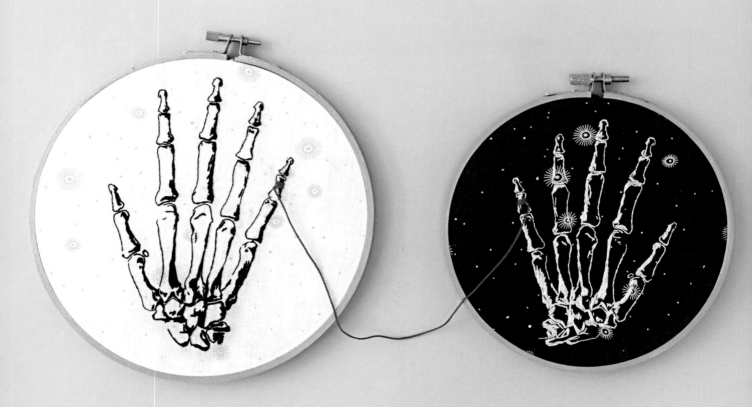

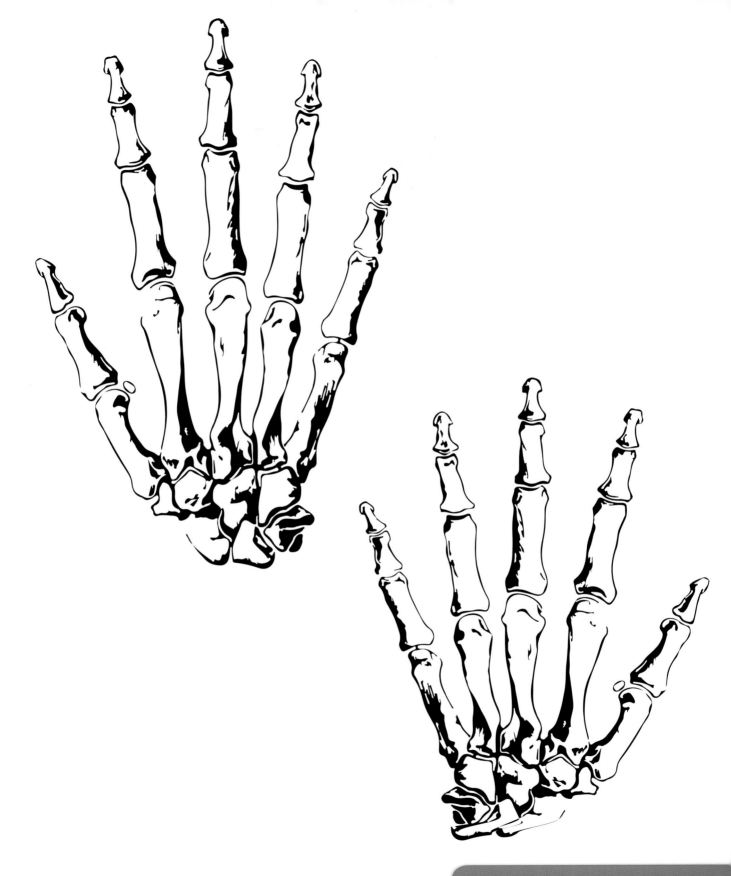

# Woodland Animals Nursery Art

These sweet little woodland creatures are darling handmade additions to a baby's nursery. Easy stitches, cute flowers, and fun fabric make these a quick project.

## what you need

Base background fabric: 9″ × 9″ square for each animal

Cotton fabric for animal body: 4″ × 5″ for each animal (Pick your color palette first; then choose the body color if not using white or a natural animal-fur color.)

Paper pattern of body outline for appliqué shapes

Wash-away pattern of full image for stitching

Sew-through fusible webbing: 4″ × 5″ for each animal

6″ wooden hoop

## How You Do It

1. Use the paper pattern (pullout page P2) to cut out the animal body and fusible webbing. Press these together.

2. Apply the animal body piece to the base fabric with a nice, hot iron. Make sure all the edges are firmly secured.

3. Apply the stitch pattern over the appliqué and stitch according to the pattern.

4. Wash off the pattern. Frame in a sweet painted hoop in a coordinating color (see Hoop It, page 21).

## Tips and Tricks

For my samples, I chose to keep the animals white so the flower crowns really stood out. I used all different stitches and colors but kept them the same between all three animals so they looked like a matching set. I outlined the animals using black perle cotton. The rest of the stitching was done in regular cotton floss.

For the flowers and leaves, I used a satin stitch in a light color to roughly stitch a background and then stitched the pattern over the top of the satin stitches with a darker color.

Instead of stitching the flower crowns, you could use felt to cut out the flowers and connect them with French knots or beads.

These are whimsical patterns, so experiment with whimsical fabric choices either for the animal bodies or the background.

I did find that after soaking off the stitching pattern, the webbing had released a little bit around the edges. I used dots of craft glue and pressed the edges back in place.

# Pretty Butterflies

Stitching on tulle is very popular because it looks like your work is floating! Use thread-sketch techniques with beautiful variegated silk thread to highlight the beauty and art of butterfly wings.

## what you need

Tulle: 6˝ × 6˝ for most sizes, 8˝ × 8˝ for largest butterfly

Embroidery hoop: 4˝ as shown, 6˝ for largest butterfly

Hot glue

Coordinating felt, if framing in the hoop: ³⁄₈˝ × inner circumference of hoop

Silk thread (*optional*)

## How You Do It

1. Place the pattern (pullout page P2) onto the tulle. Hoop the tulle fairly tightly. Be careful to keep the tension even, as tulle is a net of fine plastic and will stretch out and tear.

2. Stitch the outline using a double running stitch. This makes the stitching the same on the front and the back and will keep the outline clean and easy to fill.

3. After the outlines, veins, and any other guiding lines are stitched, wash off the pattern. Let dry and re-hoop it.

**4.** Fill the outline. You can either fill in each little block created by the veins or spill the color over multiple blocks. This is the fun part! Look online for inspiration, or pick your favorite colors and go for it.

**5.** Finish the hoop using the desired finish (see Hoop It, page 21). After gluing all the edges down, I take one extra finishing step because tulle is see-through and everything shows. Glue a thin strip of felt around the inside edge to cover any unsightly glue and edges.

## Tips and Tricks

For my two samples, I used Silk 'n Colors variegated thread from The ThreadGatherer. This is a twelve-ply silk floss that is really gorgeous and shiny. For the blue-and-red butterfly, I used a single strand for the whole thing. For the bright pink-and-turquoise butterfly, I used two strands. I like both equally well and will probably stick to two strands if I do them again because it was a little faster.

I originally only used one piece of tulle but found that the weave was just too loose to properly hold the threads. So I added a different second piece on top where the mesh had smaller holes. Putting them together made stitching much easier, and I was able to get the stitches where I needed them to be for sharp edges and clean lines.

It took a bit of practice to get the feel for stitching on such open material. I found that the outline held together better and tighter if I created a chain by stabbing through just the end of the previous stitch instead of backstitching.

Use a double running stitch for the outline. The backstitch was a disaster for stitching! It looks the same on the finished project, but stitching through all the trailing threads and trying to discern them from the top threads on see-through fabric was enough to make me insane!

Use lace instead of tulle. This will give a really neat texture!

When stitching on tulle, the back of your work becomes super important. No trailing threads, no stitches out of place, no untucked ends. Time to make your grandma proud!

I left the white parts of the pattern blank so the wall would show through, but you can fill the background with stitching if you like.

# Mandala Dream Catcher

Dream catchers are a long-standing Native American tradition. They usually consist of a willow hoop with a spiderweb design in the center. Legend says that the web traps the bad dreams and lets the happy dreams through to glide down the feathers to the sleeping person below. This project is an embroidery take on a classic design. Sweet dreams!

## what you need

### For hoop

7″ hoop

Base background fabric: 10″ × 10″ square

Hot glue and glue gun

Coordinating paint for hoop (optional)

### For streamers

The following are all suggestions. If you don't have these items, that's okay! Dream catchers were made from bits and pieces of everyday life.

Approximately 1-yard lengths of:

Coordinating yarn

Ribbon

Lace

Strips of scrap fabric

Strips of tulle

Beads

Charms

Feathers

## How You Do It

1. Apply the pattern (pullout page P2) to the fabric.

2. Use the diagram to stitch the mandala pattern. Feel free to alter stitches and colors as you like.

3. Wash away the pattern and set the mandala fabric aside to dry.

4. Paint the hoop a coordinating color (see Hoop It, page 21). Set aside the hoop to let it dry completely.

5. Prepare the streamers! Gather yarn, tulle, ribbons, lace, charms … anything that you want to hang from your dream catcher. For the ribbons and yarn, cut the pieces twice as long as you want them to dangle down; you will fold them in half and slip tie them to the hoop. The project shown has streamers cut to 36″, so there would be about 17″ hanging. Add the streamers to the hoop until you are satisfied with the loveliness.

6. Finish the outside hoop (see Hoop It, page 21) and loosen the screw on the hoop. Make sure the streamers are lying mostly flat on the inside edge so it fits over the mandala fabric.

7. Use the instructions in Hoop It (page 21) to finish framing your mandala, while keeping the streamers clear of the glue.

8. Straighten the streamers and hang on the wall!

## Tips and Tricks

When I made my streamers, I started by slip tying four pieces of pale pink tulle to the outside hoop. I attached two charms I had lying around to different pieces of yarn and tied those to the hoop. I shortened these from 16″ to about 10″ and 12″ because I wanted them to hang in the middle.

I took three doubled-up lengths of yarn and made a braid, to which I attached a leaf charm in the middle. I used three coordinating colors of ribbon and tied them to the hoop. I just kept adding until I felt there were lots of pretty streams to assist the good dreams!

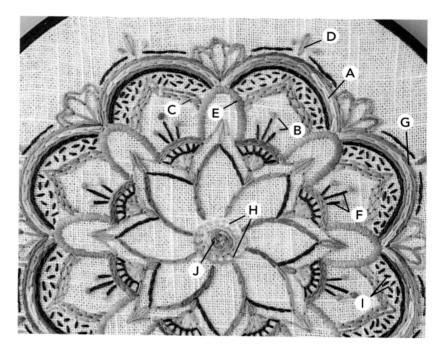

A. Chain Stitch

B. French Knots

C. Backstitch

D. Lazy Daisy

E. Satin Stitch

F. Split Stitch

G. Stem Stitch

H. Blanket Stitch

I. Straight Stitch

J. Woven Wheel

# Polar Bear, Snowflakes, and Glass

Create a gorgeous wintry scene with a white polar bear accented with vintage glass beads.

## what you need

Base fabric: White or cream
10″ × 10″ square

Seed beads, bugle beads, crystals,
and so on in wintery colors

Thread for stitching

Coordinating thread to match
the beads

Beading needle

8″ wooden hoop

## How You Do It

1. Apply the pattern (pullout page P2) to the fabric. Stitch the pattern. Use various colors of blues and grays to stitch the details as marked on the pattern with solid lines.

2. See the instruction in Pile on the Glitz (page 36) to add lines of beads to the snowflakes and finish off the detailed inside of the bear. Get creative; experiment with the beads that you have in your stash.

3. For the snowflakes, use a white or silver metallic thread and get creative with scallop stitches, straight stitches, and bead accents.

4. Wash off the pattern and let it dry.

5. Finish the hoop, following the instructions in Hoop It (page 21).

## Tips and Tricks

In my hoop, the outline of the bear is done in a stem stitch with three strands of regular floss. The inside details use two strands. The charcoal stitching is a gorgeous charcoal metallic fine braid by Kreinik. The snowflakes are stitched in white iridescent and silver ultrafine braid by Kreinik. The middle snowflake uses a scallop stitch (a lazy daisy with the ends spread apart) to make the gentle curves.

I used fine white-gold glitter to cover my hoop—just to be extra sparkly!

Try other color palettes that may not instantly be termed "wintry," like blush pink and sage, peach and teal, or even a perfect, clean all white.

This project uses beads—I like to think of them as sparkling snow. You don't need beads, though. All could be all done in clean thread colors or metallic thread.

# About the Author

Alicia Burstein grew up in the great Pacific Northwest in a tiny house, where her mom ran a day care for as long as she can remember. To keep Alicia busy, her mom taught her to cross-stitch by the age of seven. Despite her undoubtedly short attention span, Alicia picked up the love of needlework, and to this day, her thread organizer is still one of her favorite possessions.

Alicia went to college and graduated twice, became a mom three times, became a nurse and a college instructor, and self-published four coloring books available on Amazon.

She loves to make pretty much anything and has dabbled in almost everything—from paint to needlework, crochet to stamping, embroidery to stained glass. She cannot knit. *At all.*

Alicia currently resides in the Bay Area with her husband and all the kids.

**Follow Alicia on social media!**

**Instagram:** @deann52
@detailsclothing

**Contact Alicia:**

**Email:** deann52@gmail.com

# Want even more creative content?

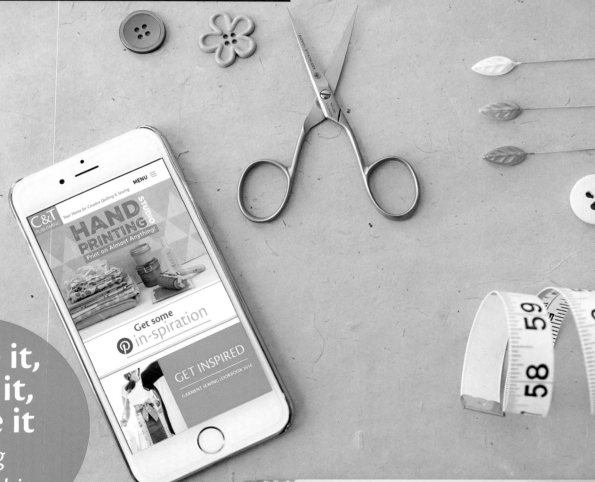

Make it,
snap it,
share it
*using*
#ctpublishing